INSTANT LESSONS

FOR SUPPLY TEACHERS

Candy Adler

9-11 YEARS

A & C Black • London

Dedicated to my Mum who would have been so proud!

I would like to personally thank the following people for their contributions to this book in one way or another:
My son, Lee; My lovely Dad, Arnie, and Gill; Pat Woodcock-Howes; Sharon Laming – la mia amica bella; the very talented Katie Collins; Deputy Head and teacher extraordinaire, Koula Christofides-Quinn; Alan Cocker and all the staff and children at Cranborne Primary School, Potters Bar, Herts; Laura Schofield at Capita Education Resourcing (Luton branch); Dawn King; Bob, Mandy and Alan at the Cock o' the North, Bell Bar, Herts for all the cappuccini, backchat, laughter, encouragement and allowing me to spread my work all over the tables; everyone else who has helped me along the way.

Published 2009 by A & C Black Publishers Limited
36 Soho Square, London W1D 3QY
www.acblack.com

ISBN 978-1-4081-1159-8

Copyright text: © Candy Adler 2009
Copyright illustrations: © Catherine Ward 2009
Copyright cover illustration: © KJA Artists 2009
Editor: Margot O'Keeffe
Designed by: Blade Communications
CD-ROM designed and developed by Cambridge Digital (www.cambridgedigital.com); produced by Will Burrows

A CIP catalogue record for this book is available from the British Library.

The author and publishers gratefully acknowledge permission to reproduce the following copyright material:

Blake Education Publishers for the text "Simply Solar: Asteroids, Meteoroids and Comets" from Go Facts Space: The Solar System © 2006

Cavendish Music (Publisher) for:
THE FOUR SEASONS by Vivaldi (Composer): Winter (Largo) and Spring (Allegro)
THE CARNIVAL OF THE ANIMALS by Saint Saens (Composer): Aquarium; Album CAV ASV 665 Organ Symphony etc Batiz Track No. 9 The Carnival of the Animals – The Elephant
© Noel Petty for 'Water cycle'
Peters Fraser and Dunlop (www.pfd.co.uk) on behalf of Roger McGough for 'The Sound Collector' by Roger McGough from Pillow Talk (© Roger McGough 1990)
Rijksmuseum, Amsterdam for 'Entrance Gate to a Farm with Haystacks' by Vincent Van Gogh

Shutterstock for:
Design a Clock Resource Sheet
Pendulum clock (2522276), Alexander Sakhatovsky; Traditional ornate clock (997947), Arturo Limon; Traditional zodiac clock (22815328), Desmond D; Cuckoo clock (11914117), Marc Dietrich; Modern art clock (5823529), Franck Boston; Digital fridge clock (25697575), ironi; Novelty seed clock (2844292), coka; Novelty fork/spoon clock (9550588), Tatiana Popova; Novelty diet clock (11758777), Gorilla; Novelty frog clock (3105278), Marek Szumlas; Novelty globe clock (14213977), jon le-bon; Novelty books clock (14307067), vsilvek
Simply Solar Resource Sheet
Comet passing Earth (23278099), Reef; Meteor crater in Arizona (14593780), Paul B Moore

Printed and bound in Great Britain by Caligraving Ltd, Thetford, Norfolk

A & C Black uses paper produced with elemental chlorine-free pulp, harvested from managed sustainable forests.

Instant Lessons for Supply Teachers

The job of the supply teacher is one of the most challenging in education. Supply teachers are expected, at short notice, to enter a classroom full of unfamiliar pupils and to deliver inclusive lessons that take account of pupils with differing abilities and that engage them all in worthwhile, curriculum-relevant learning experiences.

The *Instant Lessons for Supply Teachers* series offers a bank of lesson plans and reproducible resources across the curriculum, which can be used at a moment's notice by teachers providing emergency cover. There are three books, one each for 5–7 year olds, 7–9 year olds and 9–11 year olds. Each of these provides 30 lesson plans – 10 Literacy, 10 Mathematics and 10 spread across the other areas of learning (Science, History, Geography, Art, Design, Music, PE and PSHE).

Each book is accompanied by a CD-ROM with all the resources needed – ready-to-print, so there's no need to carry around multiple books and bulky materials. In addition, the CD-ROMs contain PowerPoint versions of all the lesson plans so they can be displayed for whole-class use on an interactive whiteboard.

About the books

Each book contains:
- An introduction explaining how the resources are organised.
- Practical tips and essential information for supply teachers.
- A lesson-plan for each of the 30 lessons. Each of these is presented in a unique and easy-to-use grid format.

The lessons are not numbered as it is not intended that they should be done in a specific order, but rather that they should be dipped into and chosen as appropriate to the needs of the class. It is envisaged that each lesson will take about one hour unless otherwise stated.

- One of the reproducible sheets that accompany the lesson, to give you a glimpse, as you read the lesson plan, of how the resources support the lesson. That sheet as well as all other sheets can be found on the CD-ROM.
- Answers, as appropriate, to lesson-plan activities.

Overview of the CD-ROMs

For each lesson in the book, the CD-ROM contains:
- A PowerPoint presentation of the lesson plan for using on an interactive whiteboard
- The Lesson-Plan Grid
- A list of Success Criteria
- Reproducible and customisable Resource and Activity Sheets
- Where appropriate, colour Resource Sheets for display on an interactive whiteboard
- For some lessons (e.g. Music, PE/Dance), audio files of music
- Some Generic Resources for general use within the Maths section
- The pages of this book as a PDF for viewing and printing out.

For further information, please see page 6 'How to use the CD-ROM'.

Sample lesson-plan grid

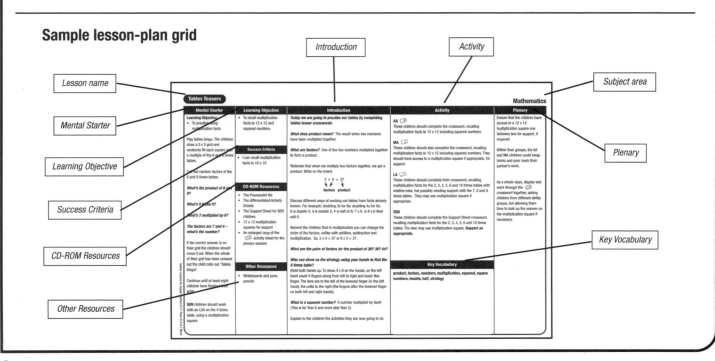

The lesson-plan grids (see facing page)

Each grid provides:

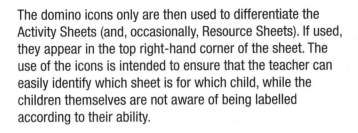

- Learning Objective/s
- Success Criteria
- A list of the CD-ROM Resources required
- A list of Other Resources required
- An Introduction to the lesson, to be used with the whole class
- Description of the group, paired or individual Activity for different levels of ability
- A Key Vocabulary word bank
- Ideas for a Plenary session

In addition:

- All Mathematics lesson-plan grids have a Mental Starter section.
- All Literacy lesson-plan grids in *Instant Lessons for Supply Teachers 5-7 Years* have a Phonics Starter section.

Differentiation

Where relevant, ideas are provided for differentiating the content of the lesson to suit the needs of the different abilities in a class. When differentiation by task is suggested, the notes in the Activity section of the lesson-plan grid are organised under the following headings with accompanying domino icons:

AA
The suggestions here are for children with an above average ability, or at the top end of the book's age range.

MA
The suggestions here are for children of average ability, or in the middle of the book's age range.

LA
The suggestions here are for children of lower ability, or at the lower end of the book's age range.

SEN
Usually the children with Special Education Needs are given the same task as the LA children. However, occasionally added support for these children is necessary.

The domino icons only are then used to differentiate the Activity Sheets (and, occasionally, Resource Sheets). If used, they appear in the top right-hand corner of the sheet. The use of the icons is intended to ensure that the teacher can easily identify which sheet is for which child, while the children themselves are not aware of being labelled according to their ability.

The reproducible sheets

Activity Sheets
Activity Sheets are those sheets on which the children will be inputting information in some form. This may be writing, completing tables or creating designs and artwork. These sheets are differentiated where possible and this is shown using the dominoes icons described above.

Support Activity Sheets
These sheets are for children who need additional support.

Resource Sheets
Resource Sheets are non-consumable sheets. They are not intended for the children to write on. It is recommended that they are displayed on the whiteboard or enlarged copies printed out and displayed somewhere in the classroom. In some cases, these are provided in full colour. Many of the Resource Sheets are gameboards. In some cases, they are also differentiated so that the children play the game most suited to their ability, even though it has the same objective as the other gameboard(s) for other ability groups. Again, these could be enlarged and laminated. In some cases, the rules are on the gameboard itself and, in other cases, the rules are a separate Resource Sheet to be displayed or for the children to keep with them. It is recommended that you explain or read through any game rules with the children; the reading level of the written rules may not be accessible to all children.

Generic Sheets
The CD-ROM contains a collection of Generic Sheets within the Maths section:

- Number lines: 0–100, 0–50 and 0–20
- Playing cards for the numbers 1 to 10
- Playing cards for the numbers 11 to 20
- Playing cards for the numbers 21 to 30
- Multiplication squares
- 100 squares
- Numbers Word Bank

It would be useful to have these laminated so that they can be used many times, rather than printing off several sheets.

Supply Teacher Feedback Form

The Supply Teacher Feedback Form on page 72 (and also on the CD-ROM) provides a helpful template on which to feed back information to the class teacher. A filled-in exemplar is provided on page 73 of this book.

Answers

Answers to activities are provided as appropriate, both at the back of this book (on pages 74–80) and on the CD-ROM along with the other resources for the relevant lesson unit.

The PowerPoint presentations

The PowerPoint presentations offer you an alternative method of delivering the lesson. As you talk the class through the various points, a frame-by-frame version of the lesson, together with any diagrams or sample sheets needed to demonstrate the activity, is displayed.

You can move down the points by clicking on the screen or using the page down key on the keyboard. Note that a small red + sign indicates that there is more text to follow on that slide.

The Success Criteria sheet features towards the end of the presentation – before the Plenary session – so that it can be left on display for the children to refer to as they work.

How to use the CD-ROM

The CD-ROM included with this book contains an easy-to-use interface that allows to you to print out pages from the book, to view them (e.g. on an interactive whiteboard) or to customise the activities to suit the needs of your pupils.

Getting started
Insert the CD-ROM into your CD drive and the disk should autorun and launch the interface in your web browser. If the disk does not autorun, open 'My Computer' and select the CD drive, then open the file 'start.exe'. If you are using a Mac, select the CD drive and open the 'start.app' file.

Please note: due to the differences between Mac and PC fonts, you may experience some unavoidable variations in typography and page layouts.

Navigating through the CD-ROM

The Home Screen provides links to the following areas of the CD-ROM: the End User Licence Agreement, the Supply Teacher Feedback Form, and the main menu or Contents Page.

Four options are available to you from the Contents page:

1. The first option takes you to the Book PDF, where you can choose pages of the book to view and print out, using Adobe Reader (see below).

2. The second option takes you to the Mathematics lessons resources.

3. The third option takes you to the Literacy lessons resources.

4. The fourth option takes you to the Other Subjects lessons resources.

Click on any of options 2–4 to display a list of the 10 lessons in the relevant section. Then click on a lesson title to display all the resources for that lesson.

There is a 'Back' button in the top right of the Contents screen to return to the Home Screen.

If you do not have the Microsoft Office suite (with Word and PowerPoint), you might like to consider using OpenOffice instead. This is a multi-platform and multilingual office suite, and an 'open-source' project. It is compatible with all other major office suites, and the product is free to download, use and distribute (see www.openoffice.org). Other compatible software includes Ability Office and Star Office. Use an Internet search engine to locate current versions of alternative software.

If you do not already have Adobe Reader (for accessing PDF files) it can be downloaded for free from www.adobe.com.

File formats

You will find four different file formats on the CD-ROM:

- PowerPoint files (PPT) enabling the lessons to be presented on an interactive whiteboard;

- MP3 files containing music tracks for Music and PE/Dance lessons*;

- PDF files of all resources enabling them to be viewed, displayed on an interactive whiteboard or visualiser, and printed;

- WORD files of many of the resources, enabling you to edit and customise the resource – and to print it out, or copy and paste it into your existing planning using Microsoft Word.

*NB: This CD-ROM cannot be used in a CD player. The audio tracks on the CD-ROM are provided in mp3 format. These can be copied from CD or computer onto a media player such as an mp3 player, or copied to a new CD to use in a CD player for personal or educational use. No rights of distribution are granted or implied by this.

Technical support

If you have any question regarding the *Instant Lessons for Supply Teachers* software, please email us at the address below. We will get back to you as quickly as possible.

educationalsales@acblack.com

Example Lesson Resources: Dictionary Challenge

The following is an example of a lesson with the resources provided.

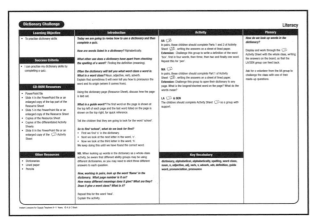

Lesson Plan Grid

Success Criteria Sheet

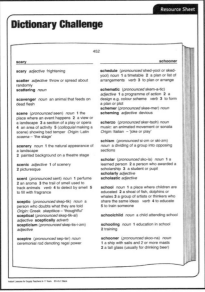

Resource Sheet

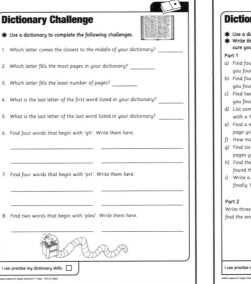

Activity Sheet

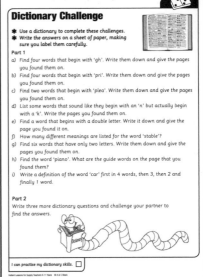

Activity Sheet

Getting Started

Types of supply-teaching work

There are generally three different types of supply-teaching work available:

- Day-to-day work involves covering sickness, training courses, conferences and so on. In the case of sickness, this type of work usually involves last-minute, early-morning calls. Cover for conferences and training courses is most often pre-booked.

- Longer-term work may involve any cover from a week to a half term (6-8 weeks).

- Fixed contract may involve cover for between a half term to an academic year – to cover long-term sickness, maternity leave and so on.

Ways of getting supply work

Local Education Authority (LEA)

To obtain supply teaching work through your Local Education Authority, you must register with them. The procedure will differ from LEA to LEA. If your work comes via an LEA, you should be paid to scale and have pension options through your relevant county. Payment is usually made through their own payroll. Rules of employment vary between LEAs, so check with whichever covers the areas in which you wish to work for their individual conditions and rules.

Agencies

Before registering with an agency, it is valuable to seek recommendations. Talking to other supply teachers is a good place to start. Additionally, schools often have a favourite agency to which they are loyal, so if you wish to work in particular schools, try to find out which agencies they use. You might wish to register with several in order to get sufficient work. However, be aware that agencies set their own rates of pay and this is usually less than LEAs.

Directly through schools

You can only be employed by a school if you already have an LEA payroll number which requires registration with the LEA.

In all cases, you will need to have a Criminal Records Bureau (CRB) Disclosure form. The LEA, agency or school should be able to advise you on obtaining and completing the form.

Preparation

What do I take to school with me?

- ✔ This book and the accompanying CD-ROM
- ✔ A project file containing hard copies from the CD-ROM of relevant lesson plans, Resource Sheets and Activity Sheets
- ✔ Your CRB form, a photo ID card if you have one and your GTC registration card
- ✔ Bottled water (This is sometimes charged for, as are hot drinks. You should offer to pay for any refreshments you have.)
- ✔ Lunch (although it is often possible to order and purchase a lunch if you do it by break time)
- ✔ A story or poetry book (as a filler or for the end of the day)
- ✔ Coloured pens (check the school's policy on marking the register and children's work)
- ✔ Sticky tack (for the Success Criteria and other display material)
- ✔ Counters and dice for the games
- ✔ Trainers to change into if you have to take a PE lesson
- ✔ A small book to keep details of lesson times, names of the Headteacher and other staff and any other relevant notes for future visits
- ✔ Stickers as a reward for good work or behaviour
- ✔ Timesheet – without it you won't get paid!

When should I arrive?

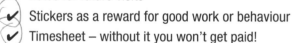

If you say you are available for work, you should be up and ready to go. Schools really appreciate your arriving early, so estimate how long it will take you to get there and be sure to plan your route. Being prepared before the children arrive is paramount to a successful first impression. Ideally you should aim to arrive at least 30 minutes before the start of school.

What should I wear?

Dress professionally, but comfortably. There is an unwritten dress code, which means that jeans and track suits are not acceptable, unless, of course, you are given prior permission to wear these for PE. Wear footwear that you can take PE in or take trainers with you to change into. If you are female, avoid low necklines and short skirts.

What do I do when I get there?

Not all of the following issues need to be addressed as soon as you arrive. However, if you are able to get there early enough to do so, it will make life a lot easier!

- You will have to sign the visitor's book and offer your CRB and identification.
- You may or may not be shown the staff room and the toilets – if not, ask.
- Check whether there is an interactive whiteboard (IWB) in your classroom. If yes, check that it is connected to a laptop or computer and that it is working. If not, you will need hard copies of everything you need for your lessons.
- Find the timetable. Often there is a copy on the wall for the children. This will tell you what the routines are and what time things like assembly are. You should assume you are to attend.
- Fire drill instructions are usually displayed. Make sure you know where the meeting point is.

If you are not told, ask:

- whether you are on break duty – if the class teacher for whom you are covering is on duty, you will probably be expected to do their duty (a list is usually on a board in the staffroom);
- if you stay in the classroom during wet play or will be relieved;
- whether any planning has been left for you (if it has, read it through so that if there are any problems, you have time to query it and/or use the photocopier);
- whether there are any children of whom you need to be especially aware (e.g. those with SENs or behaviour problems);
- what the school behaviour policy is so that you know how to react to bad behaviour;
- whether there is a bell to indicate the end of morning sessions;
- whether or not you collect the class in the morning/breaks and so on, and if so, from where;
- whether or not you lead children out at the end of the day or wait for parents to collect them.

Many classrooms have a Teaching Assistant (TA) assigned to them for at least part of the day. They are a valuable resource, so use them! Not only will they support your teaching, but they are also a treasure trove of information with regard to the individual children, ability groups, the class, school routines and rules, and, very importantly, where the resources are kept. (Be aware: headteachers often ask teaching assistants for feedback about you!)

What will the school expect of me?

Schools expect a supply teacher who will provide professional teaching cover with the minimum disruption to the class and school routine. If work has been left by the class teacher, then it must be taught! However, there may be occasions where you are unable to do so due to lack of resources required or understanding of the planning. In these incidences, use your own lesson plans, but ensure you note your reasons for doing so and what you taught instead on your feedback form.

In addition to effective teaching, schools will also expect you to:

- be prepared and adaptable – things change rapidly in a school day;
- have good control of the class;
- mark all work taught (see 'Marking', page 11);
- leave feedback for the class teacher (see Feedback Form, page 72);
- leave the classroom tidy, shut all windows and turn off lights, computers and the IWB projector;
- report to the office to have your timesheet signed, and sign out.

Behaviour management

Behaviour management is one of the biggest issues in primary classrooms today. You probably have your own strategies that are tried and tested, and that you use on a day-to-day basis. However, we all have different natures and teaching styles, and every catchment area is slightly different, as is every class temperament. What works with some classes or teachers won't necessarily work with others. You need to be adaptable and try different tactics until you find what works for both you and the individual class. The most important thing to remember, however frustrated or exasperated you may feel, is not to lose your temper or shout. Not only will this not result in effective class control, it is likely to exacerbate the situation, causing more problems.

If you don't enjoy teaching in a school because of continued bad behaviour, you don't need to go back. However, you should see any day through to the end. If it is really bad, then there is nothing wrong with asking for help. Other members of staff will usually be willing to offer advice, recognising that it is more difficult to control the behaviour of children you don't know.

First impressions

Children don't like changes to their routines. They need to feel safe and relaxed to be ready to learn. Show that you are in control but approachable. Preparation is the key. Have some early morning work on the board for when they enter the classroom, to keep them occupied while you are dealing with the inevitable queries and issues that arise first thing. Write the date, 'Good morning' and 'My name is ...'. Beneath this write the task; for example, 'How many small words can you make out of this word: impossible?' Other tasks might be practising spellings/tables or writing as many number sentences as possible for a chosen number (choose according to ability).

Establishing your expectations from the outset

- Smile but be authoritative when you speak.
- Select sensible children to help you with any important morning jobs, such as taking the register to the office.
- Appoint a helper of the day.
- Lay down your main class rules as soon as possible and give the children a clear idea of your expectations for the day.
- Request silence for the register, and ask the children to respond to their name by answering and giving a little wave so that you can put a face to the name.

Making it personal

The sooner you know the children's names, the better. This puts them at ease and helps with class control. Try giving each child a sticky label with their name on it to wear. Your teaching assistant may be able to find the sticky labels and do this for you. Or you can carry some in your supply kit, just in case. Alternatively, you could give the children an A4 sheet of paper to fold horizontally and write their first names in large, clear letters so that you can see it from the front of the class.

Putting them at their ease

We all like to know what we are likely to be doing for the day, so tell the children what you have planned. Try to praise them often as possible. Comment on how patiently children are sitting or waiting to speak and acknowledge the efforts some children make in trying to answer a question even if the answer is wrong. Good behaviour that is being noticed and rewarded can be contagious!

Remember to give the children 'settling in' time. Many of them will try to test you. Equally, many children will be very wary of you; after all, you are an 'unknown quantity'.

Children with special needs

Special needs may range from ADHD to dyslexia, dyspraxia, autism and learning difficulties. The

Headteacher or other staff will usually make a point of providing you with information on such children. These children will need activities that are related to what the other children in the class are doing but at their ability level so they can achieve success like everyone else. If their needs are very different, there is usually a Learning Support Assistant (LSA) to support them. They can be a great help in adapting your suggested activities. By all means give special needs children jobs to boost their self-esteem, but sometimes it is just giving them the correct level of work that can produce the best behaviour, especially if it is really interesting to them.

Sanctions

Be aware of the school's behaviour and sanctions policy. Don't make threats you can't carry out or the children will not take the threat seriously next time. Make sure that the children know your expectations regarding behaviour and aim to keep them high but in a positive way.

Stop, look and listen

Children like to chat when they are supposed to be working and the noise level in a classroom needs to remain at a workable level. If a teacher becomes louder to make her/himself heard, the children tend to get louder still. Shouting (unless you have a reason to be very angry) is never successful.

Some useful strategies are:
- Say quietly 'If you can hear me, put your hand on your head'. It is surprising how quickly the class catches on!
- Try touching your head, then shoulders and so on. Children are quick to copy you, thereby helping you to gain whole-class attention in a short time.
- Use an instrument, such as a shaker, tambourine or little drum, to catch the class' attention.
- Try using signs: for example, an ear for 'listen', a red traffic light for 'stop talking', dimming or turning the lights on or off to get children's attention.
- Standing with arms folded, exaggeratedly looking at the clock or watch, until silence prevails can take quite a while, but it does work.
- Use a timer, counting up. Explain, 'If you waste my time, I'll waste yours. This is coming out of your break/lunchtime.' It is amazing how quickly it works. Always give them a chance to earn the time back!

Explain activities and keep children on task

It is important to position yourself in the classroom so that all the children can see you (and you them). When explaining a task, ask several children to repeat it. Be aware that some children with special educational needs might need instructions simplified and given one at a time. They may not be able to remember a list.

Set a time limit in which to complete work. Again, the timer could be used for this. If you are not working with a particular group, circulate around the classroom, commenting on good work or application, and helping where needed. If children have their hands up for help and you are already helping someone, tell them to ask their study partner/work buddy/person sitting next to them for help, and that you will be over shortly.

Serious incidents

Any serious incidents should be reported to the Headteacher or Deputy Head, whether they be behavioural or something a child has disclosed to you in confidence. In the case of the latter, do not encourage the child by asking questions and do not, under any circumstances, show a reaction or promise not to tell anyone else.

Do not restrain fighting children. Try blowing a whistle to shock them to attention, and send another child for help, according to the school policy, in order to protect yourself from allegations and from injuries. In the case of a child who is behaving in a way that might endanger any of the children, act in accordance with the school policy. In the absence of that, usher the rest of the class out to the nearest classroom. Under no circumstances should you make any bodily contact with a child when reprimanding them. This could be interpreted as assault, even if you have only touched their arm.

Safety issues

In order to keep the children and yourself safe while working in a school, remember:

- to be familiar with and follow the school guidelines if there is a fire;
- to follow safety guidelines during P.E. lessons – for example, children should:
  - remove all jewellery and cover any earrings that cannot be removed;
  - wear shoes when walking to and from the hall;
- not to give the children anything to eat or drink of your own.

Assessment

A supply teacher undertaking long-term cover is likely to have been given the class teacher's planning to follow and will be expected to carry out more detailed assessments. The lessons in this book are intended for use when doing varied daily supply teaching, so the only assessment will be during the lesson with questioning and marking the work.

Assessment for learning, or formative assessment, is diagnostic, usually oral, through asking questions and discussion. It is already present in the lesson plans in this book in the form of key questions within the Introduction and Plenary sessions. As you circulate, ask children specific questions about their work, for example: How did you know that? How did you get that answer? How did you work that out? What strategy did you use? Why do you think that is? What do you think you need to do next?

Don't forget to praise and give constructive feedback to move the children forward in order that they make progress.

Assessment of learning, or summative assessment, will be carried out primarily through marking. The 'I can…' success-criteria statements at the bottom of most Activity Sheets are intended for children to complete themselves to support self-assessment.

Marking

All work must be marked – it is part of your job and is usually incorporated into the contract you signed. Marking must be finished before you leave the class.

All schools have a marking policy, often displayed on the wall for the children. A glance through the books will tell you how the teacher marks and in what colour. Only mark to the learning objective set. If it is to write rhyming couplets and the couplets don't rhyme, then the learning objective has clearly not been achieved. You may wish to correct a few of the most commonly misspelled words. Maths and literacy should include a comment to help the children improve. For example, if, when marking co-ordinates, the child has omitted brackets, you could write: 'Good work, X, but remember to place brackets round each set of co-ordinates.'

What do I do at the end of the day?

✔ Leave time at the end of the day so that the children can clear up.

✔ Ask the children whether they stack the chairs, put them up on the tables or leave them.

✔ Complete any marking.

✔ Fill in the Feedback Form (see page 72).

✔ Check that the computers and projector are turned off, close the windows and turn out the lights.

✔ Get your timesheet signed, sign out and, if appropriate, give some verbal feedback to the Headteacher or secretary.

Tables Teaser Puzzles

Mental Starter	Learning Objective	Introduction	Activity	Plenary

Mental Starter

Learning Objective
- To practise using multiplication facts

Play Tables Bingo. The children draw a 3 x 3 grid and randomly fill each square with a multiple of the 6 and 8 times tables, such as 42.

Call out random factors of the 6 and 8 times tables:

What's the product of 6 and 8?

What's 9 times 8?

What's 7 multiplied by 6?

The factors are 7 and 6 – what's the number?

If the correct answer is on their grid, the children should cross it out. When the whole of their grid has been crossed out, the child calls out 'Tables Bingo!'

Continue until at least eight children have finished their grids.

SEN children should work with an LSA on the 4 times table, using a multiplication square.

Learning Objective
- To recall multiplication facts to 10 x 10 (or 12 x 12 and squared numbers)

Success Criteria
- I can recall multiplication facts to 10 x 10 (or 12 x 12 and squared numbers).

CD-ROM Resources
- PowerPoint file
- Copies of the differentiated Activity Sheets
- Copies of Generic Sheet 5 – 10 x 10 multiplication squares
- Copies of Generic Sheet 6 – 12 x 12 multiplication squares for the Plenary session
- Slide 11 in the PowerPoint file or an enlarged copy of the ⚅ Activity Sheet for the Plenary session
- Copy of the Answers Sheet

Other Resources
- Whiteboards and pens
- Pencils

Introduction

Today we are going to practise our tables by completing Tables Teaser puzzles.

What does product mean? The result when two numbers have been multiplied together.

What is a factor? One of the two numbers multiplied together to form a product.

Reiterate that when we multiply two factors together, we get a product. Write on the board:

$$3 \times 9 = 27$$
factors   product

Discuss different ways of working out tables from facts already known. For example: doubling 3s for 6s; doubling 4s for 8s; 6 is double 3; 4 is double 2; 4 is half of 8; 7 x 6 is 6 x 6 then add 6.

Remind the children that in multiplication (like addition, but unlike subtraction and division), you can change the order of the factors. So, 4 x 9 = 36 or 9 x 4 = 36.

What are the pairs of factors for the products of:
36? 3 x 12, 12 x 3, 9 x 4, 4 x 9, 6 x 6
30? 3 x 10, 10 x 3, 5 x 6, 6 x 5
44? 4 x 11, 11 x 4

Who can show us the strategy using your hands to find the 9 times table?

Hold your hands up. Let's do 3 x 9. Count 3 fingers along from left to right, beginning with left hand. Lower that finger. The tens are to the left of the lowered finger, the units to the right of the lowered finger.
(This is for Year 6 and more able Year 5.)

What is a squared number? A number multiplied by itself.

Explain the activity. Ensure the children understand how to do crossword-type puzzles.

Activity

AA ⚅
These children should complete the puzzle, recalling multiplication facts to 12 x 12 including squared numbers.

MA ⚅
These children should also complete the puzzle, recalling multiplication facts to 12 x 12 including squared numbers. They should have access to a multiplication square for support if appropriate.

LA ⚅
These children should complete their puzzle, recalling multiplication facts for the 2, 3, 4, 5, 6 and 10 times tables with relative ease, but possibly needing support with the 7, 8 and 9 times tables. They may use a multiplication square for support if appropriate.

SEN ⚅
These children should complete the Support Activity Sheet puzzle, recalling multiplication facts for the 2, 3, 4, 5, 6 and 10 times tables. The also may use a multiplication square. **Support as appropriate.**

Key Vocabulary

product, factors, numbers, multiplication, squared, square numbers, double, half, strategy

---

Plenary

Ensure that the children have access to a 12 x 12 multiplication square, one between two for support if required.

Within their groups, the AA and MA children could swap books and peer mark their partner's work.

As a whole class, display and work through the ⚅ puzzle together, asking children from different ability groups, but allowing them time to look up the answer on a multiplication square if necessary.

Display the Answers Sheet for them to study at leisure.

Tables Teaser Puzzle

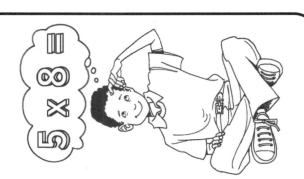

Across

1. 11 x 11
3. 8 x 12
4. 12 x 9
6. 5 x 8
7. 12 x 6
8. 6 x 4
9. 10 x 7
10. 12 x 7
11. 7 x 3
13. 5^2
15. 11 x 10
17. 12 x 11
20. 7^2
23. 2^2
24. 8^2
25. 7 x 5
27. 7 x 1
30. 6 x 0
31. 6 x 8
33. 5 x 9
34. 9 x 3
35. 3^2
36. 7 x 4

Down

1. 4^2
2. 12^2
4. 12 x 10
5. 9^2
7. 7 x 11
8. 12 x 2
10. 11 x 8
11. 3 x 7
12. 10^2
14. 8 x 7
15. 3 x 6
16. 7 x 3
18. 6^2
19. 4 x 6
21. 11 x 9
22. 9 x 7
26. 6 x 9
28. 5 x 7
29. 7 x 6
32. 8 x 11
33. 4 x 12

I can recall multiplication facts to 12 x 12 and squared numbers. ☐

Probability Sorted

Mental Starter	Learning Objective	Introduction	Activity	Plenary
Learning Objective • To count from any given number in decimal steps, extending beyond zero when counting backwards Ask the children to count on from 1 to 4 in steps of 0.2 (1, 1.2, 1.4 and so on). Then count back from 0.2 to −3 (0.2, 0, −0.2, −0.4, −0.6, −0.8, −1 and so on). Repeat this in steps of 0.25 from 15.25 to 18 and back from 0.25 to −2.25. Repeat in steps of 0.3 from 5 to 10.1 (5.3, 5.6, 5.9, 6.2, 6.5, 6.8, 7.1, 7.4 and so on) and back again.	**Learning Objective** • To describe the occurrence of familiar events using the language of chance or likelihood **Success Criteria** • I can describe events using probability language. **CD-ROM Resources** • PowerPoint file • Slide 6 in the PowerPoint file or draw a probability line (as the first example shown in the Introduction) on a whiteboard or large piece of paper • Copies of the differentiated Activity Sheets **Other Resources** Per group: • Scissors • A2 sugar paper • Ruler • Marker pen • Pens • Glue • Paper	***Today we are going to clarify the meaning of the language of probability and then sort statements by the likelihood of the events happening, using that language.*** Write the following words on the board: *certain, impossible, unlikely, likely, even chance* Draw an empty probability line beneath them as shown below. ***What does 'certain' mean?*** It is guaranteed to happen. ***What does 'impossible' mean?*** The opposite (antonym) of certain – out of the question, guaranteed not to happen. ***What does 'unlikely' mean?*** It is doubtful, improbable. ***What does 'likely' mean?*** The opposite (antonym) of unlikely – probable, expected. ***What does 'even chance' mean?*** 50/50, an equal chance of it happening, 1 in 2 chance. Ask for volunteers to label the probability line by writing the words in their correct positions. certain likely even chance unlikely impossible ***Using the words on the probability line, what are the chances of the sun rising tomorrow morning?*** Certain. Explain to the children that we know this because it happens every single day. ***Is it snowing in the Sahara Desert?*** Impossible – because it is a very hot, dry place. ***Can you suggest a statement for 'likely' and explain why it is likely?*** Repeat for unlikely and even chance. Children may find classifying events difficult, so it is important to allow time for lots of discussion of reasons for classifications. Explain the activity.	**AA** Give this group the appropriate Activity Sheet to cut up. They should elect a scribe. On A2 paper, horizontally, the scribe should draw a probability line across the top. As a group, the children should discuss each of the 20 chance statements, deciding which category it fits. The scribe should then stick each statement under the agreed heading. The children should then write **at least** two more chance statements for each heading and stick them in. **MA** Give this group the appropriate Activity Sheet. They should elect a scribe. On A2 paper, horizontally, the scribe should draw a probability line across the top. As a group, the children should discuss each of the 16 chance statements, deciding which category it fits. The scribe should then stick each statement under the agreed heading. The children should then individually, on paper, write two chance statements of their own and challenge the group to place them under the correct headings. **LA & SEN** The activity for these children is similar to above, but they should discuss, sort and stick the ten chance statements using only the headings of 'certain', 'even chance' and 'impossible'. They could then make up some new statements for each heading, scribed by the adult. **Key Vocabulary** **probability, certain, likely, even chance, unlikely, impossible, likelihood, fifty-fifty, opposite, antonym**	Work through the statements under the headings, as a class, discussing any statements that have caused confusion or 'grey areas'. Resolve any issues that have arisen during the activity. Draw a probability line on the board. Share and discuss the new statements written by the groups and write them in the agreed places on the line.

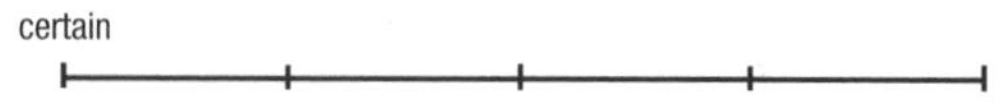

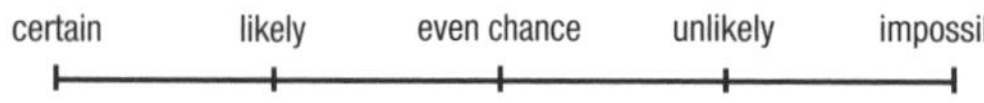

Probability Sorted

certain   likely   even chance   unlikely   impossible

Your teacher will visit Mars this year.	You will watch the television tonight.
You will go to bed before midnight tonight.	It will rain next week.
You will have a drink today.	You will go to Denmark next year.
You will have a birthday between January and December.	You will have a pet when you grow up.
You will see a real pelican on a pelican crossing.	Someone will forget part of their PE kit this week.
You will eat chips this week.	You will read a book this week.
Christmas will be in September this year.	You will drive a car when you grow up.
You will sit on a polar bear's back this week.	You will sharpen a pencil today.

Co-ordinate Pictures

Mental Starter	Learning Objective	Introduction	Activity	Plenary

Learning Objective
- To multiply and divide decimals by 10, 100 and 1000

Ask the children to write the answers to the following calculations on their individual whiteboards. They should hold up their boards with the answer after a count of ten seconds.

What is 9.4 x 10?
94.6 x 10?
946.3 x 10?
9.43 x 1000?
What is 7.43 ÷ 100?

Pose a selection of further questions, asking children to multiply and divide decimals and multiples by 10.

Learning Objective
- To plot co-ordinates

Success Criteria
- I can plot co-ordinates.

CD-ROM Resources
- PowerPoint file
- Slide 4 in the PowerPoint file or an enlarged copy of the Resource Sheet
- Copies of the Resource Sheet
- Copies of the differentiated Activity Sheets
- Copy of the Answers Sheet

Other Resources
- Whiteboards and pens
- Pencils
- Rulers

Introduction

Today we are going to make pictures using co-ordinates.

Draw a grid on the board or display the grid on the Resource Sheet. Point to the horizontal line.

What is the correct name for this line?
The Horizontal Axis. The x-axis is how we refer to the horizontal axis.

Point to the vertical line. *What is the correct name for this line?*
The Vertical Axis. The y-axis is how we refer to the vertical axis.

What is the rule for the order of co-ordinates?
Explain that when reading and plotting co-ordinates, we use: Along the corridor (along the x-axis) and up the stairs (up the y-axis). Stress, horizontal first, vertical second.

How do we write co-ordinates?
They are always in brackets, separated by a comma.

Point out that the axis numbers sit by the line and that the point indicated by the numbers in brackets at which to make the mark is always at the point of intersection of x and y.

Demonstrate reading and plotting points. Compare this with using a multiplication square.

Plot some points using crosses.
What are the co-ordinates of this point? Write them on the board. Repeat this activity several times.

Who can plot these co-ordinates?
Give out several co-ordinates and invite children to come up to the board and plot the points.

Who can explain why (3,2) is not the same as (2,3)?

Explain the activity.

Activity

Give out copies of the Resource Sheet to all the children.

AA
These children should first plot the points to reveal the 'Tardis' (from *Dr Who*) and then go on to design their own grid picture. The teacher should model making her own picture.
NB: Making your own picture is more difficult than it looks. Make the designs very simple.

MA
These children should plot the points to reveal the apple and then the number 8.

LA
These children should plot the points for 'Hi' and then the picture of the ice-cream cone. Give support if required.
Extension: Can they draw the initial of their first name and then plot the co-ordinates?

SEN
As LA. **With support.**

Key Vocabulary

axis, axes, x-axis, y-axis, vertical, horizontal, grid, numeric, co-ordinates, point of intersection, cross, plotting

Plenary

Select a good example of a picture produced by the AA group. Select as many children as needed for each to plot one of the points on the board.

When it is complete, ask the whole class to evaluate it.

Ask some of the children who plotted the co-ordinates for the initial letter of their name to call out the co-ordinates for you – or another child – to draw it on the board.

Co-ordinate Pictures

✱ Using the blank grid, plot each point given below, joining them up as you plot them USING A RULER.

✱ Stop at the end of each section and start again on the next section.

- (8,11) (9,12) (9,13) (10,14) (11,14) (12,15) (13,15) (15,16) (14,14) (14,13) (13,13) (12,12) (9,12)

Remember!
→ Along the corridor and ↑ up the stairs!

- (4,1) (11,1) (14,4) (14,8) (11,11) (9,11) (8,10) (7,10) (6,11) (4,11) (1,8) (1,4) (4,1)

- (8,11) (8,10) (7,10) (7,13) (10,16) (10,15) (8,13) (8,11)

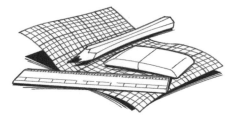

✱ Now try this one. You will need a new grid to work on.

- (9,12) (8,13) (8,15)

- (9,12) (10,13) (10,15) (8,17) (6,15) (6,13) (7,12) (6,11) (6,9) (8,7) (10,9) (10,11) (9, 12)

- (7,12) (8,11) (8,9)

- (5,18) (11,18) (11,13) (11,8) (8,6) (5,8) (5,13) (5, 18)

I can plot co-ordinates. ☐

Netball Angles

Mental Starter

Learning Objective
- To revise turns/degrees using clockwise and anti-clockwise

Ask the children to stand up and face the board. First they should guess the answers, then try them out. Then they should start by facing the whiteboard each time.

If you turned 180° anti-clockwise, what will you be facing now?

Now, turn 90° anti-clockwise (to the left), then immediately turn 360°. What are you facing now?

Now, turn 180° anti-clockwise, then immediately turn 270° clockwise. What are you facing now?

Learning Objectives
- To estimate and measure angles, using a protractor, to within 5°
- To learn to identify whether an angle is obtuse, acute or a right angle

Success Criteria
- I can estimate and measure angles using a protractor, to within 5°.

CD-ROM Resources
- PowerPoint file
- Copies of Resource Sheet ⚃ enlarged to A3 for AA and MA children
- Copy of Resource Sheet ⚁ enlarged to A3 for LA and SEN children
- Copy of the Netball Angles Score Sheet (Resource Sheet 3) for all pairs or teams

Other Resources

Per pair/team:
- Two pairs of different coloured counters
- Dice
- Protractor
- Calculator (optional for AA pairs)

Introduction

Today we are going to play the Netball Angles game.

Draw a variety of angles on the board (acute – less than 90°; obtuse – greater than 90°; right angle 90°; straight line – 180°)

Explain to the children that they are going to revise general definitions of angles.

Point to an angle. *What do you estimate this angle to be?*

What sort of angle is it?

Draw some more angles on the board.

What do you estimate this angle to be?

What sort of angle is it?

What are the rules for measuring angles with a protractor? Line up the centre of the protractor on the zero line with the vertex of the angle (the point at which the two lines of the angle meet). Move the paper around till you can measure easily.

Remind the children that they begin at zero, whether they are using the inside or the outside of the protractor. Demonstrate this.

Select some children to estimate and then measure the angles that have been drawn on the board.

If 180° is a straight line, then any angles on a straight line will total 180°.

Explain the activities the children are about to do, making it clear that the goal posts are the score sheet and players only move their counter if their answer is correct.

Activity

AA ⚃

These children should play in pairs according to the rules on Resource Sheet ⚃.

Add the following rule: Each time they have agreed an angle, the player whose turn it is should calculate what the angle is that would make the two measure up first to 180° and then to 360°. They may use a calculator to check their answers. If both are correct, the player whose turn it is may score another $\frac{1}{2}$ point.

MA ⚁

As above, without the additional rule and calculations. Give support if it is required.

LA ⚁ **& SEN**

LA and SEN children should play as two teams using the game on Resource Sheet ⚁. Both teams should check the answers given. **Give support as required.**

This game can be also be used for measuring and drawing the angles, by adapting the scoring slightly. Points are scored by drawing the correct angle (checked by a partner) and the counter is moved up to the next numbered circle.

NB: This game can be also be used for measuring and drawing the angles, by adapting the scoring slightly. Points are scored by drawing the correct angle (checked by a partner) and the counter is moved up to the next numbered circle.

Key Vocabulary

acute, obtuse, right angle, degrees, less than, greater than, estimate, protractor, set-square, vertex, point of intersection

Plenary

Remind the children that if 180° is a straight line, then any angles on a straight line will total 180°.

What operation do we use to reach a total? Addition.

What is the special symbol that shows that the angle is a right angle?

Show some angles on a straight line. (See the last slide of the Powerpoint file.)

What do we already know about these angles by looking at them? If 180° is a straight line, then any angles on a straight line will total 180°.

How can we find the missing angles? (See the Powerpoint file.)

How can we check that we are right? Use the inverse to check; namely:
? + 60° ➔ 180° – 60° = 120°
So 180° – 120° = 60°.

Netball Angles Game

- Play with a partner, taking it in turns to go.

- Place one of your two counters on START and the other beneath your goal post on the score sheet.

- Player 1 throws the dice, moves that number of spaces, estimates the angle landed on, and then measures it and identifies it as an acute, obtuse or right angle. Player 2 checks the measurement.

- Score using the goal posts: each numbered circle is ½ point and the space on the pole between the circles is ½ point.

- If your estimate is correct to within 5°, score ½ point and place your scoring counter on the pole on the goal post beneath the numbered circle (1). If you measured the angle correctly, move the counter up ½ space on the goal post.

- If both your estimate and your measurement are correct, your counter should be on the 1.

- If your answer is not correct, you do not score.

- The winning player is the first to score a goal or to reach HOME on the board.

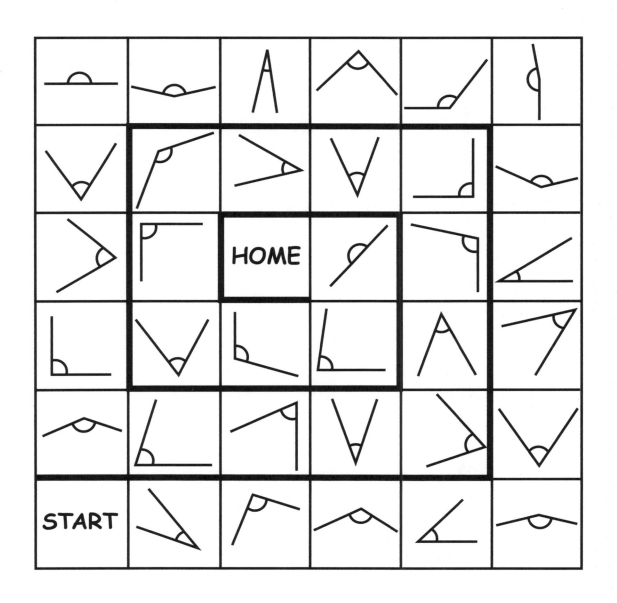

Measure Up!

Mental Starter	Learning Objective	Introduction	Activity	Plenary
Learning Objective • To convert metric lengths between units of measurements Using their whiteboards and pens, the children should write the answer to the following questions and show them after a count to ten. Write the following on the board (without the answers) and ask children to answer: 10mm = (1)cm 100cm = (1)m 1000m = (1)km Then ask: ***How many mm in a metre?*** 1000 ***How did you work it out?*** Repeat for mm in 1km (1,000,000) and cm in 1km (100,000). ***What are:*** ***360cm in m?*** 3.6m ***1.043km in cm and in mm?*** 104,300cm; 1,043,000mm Repeat with similar questions.	• To develop ability to estimate lengths accurately • To accurately measure lengths to the nearest 10mm (1cm) **Success Criteria** • I can develop the ability to estimate lengths accurately. • I can accurately measure lengths to the nearest 10mm (1cm). **CD-ROM Resources** • PowerPoint file • Copies of the differentiated Activity Sheets • Copy of the Resource Sheet (rules) **Other Resources** • Whiteboards and pens Per pair: • 2 different coloured pencils • Scissors • 30cm ruler/tape measure • 1 dice • Sticky tack to secure the arrows	***Today we are going to play a game to practise estimating lengths and then measuring them accurately.*** ***Why do we need standard measures and to measure accurately?*** So that when you buy something, it is the same length (or weight) wherever you buy it. Show your arms outstretched and compare them with the tallest child and the smallest child to demonstrate the difference and the need for a standard unit of measurement. Revise how to use rulers and tape measures. ***What are the rules to remember when using a ruler?*** Discuss in particular the issue of the 0 and where to begin measuring. Demonstrate measuring on the board. ***What are the rules to remember when using a tape measure?*** Remind the children to look at the measure first because sometimes the numbering begins right at the edge and sometimes there is a little gap or a metal edging. It is important to see where the actual zero is. Model estimating a length using the pointed end of two arrows stuck to the table with sticky tack to mark the distance between them, and then measuring the distance. ***What do you estimate the length of this book is in cm/mm?*** Select a child to measure it. Repeat this with other objects. Explain the activity.	**AA** Using Activity Sheet, these children should play the millimetre game. They estimate the length in the square they land on, marking it out on the table with the arrows stuck down with sticky tack, then measure correctly to within 5mm. Both players should check the measurements. Score accordingly (see Activity Sheet: Rules). **MA** Using Activity Sheet, these children should also play the millimetre game.They should also estimate the length, marking it out with the arrows, then measure correctly to within 10mm. Both players should check the measurements. Score accordingly (see Activity Sheet: Rules). **LA** Using Resource Sheet, these children should play the game using centimetres. They should estimate the length, marking it out with the arrows, then measure. All to check measurements. Score accordingly (see Activity Sheet: Rules). **Support if appropriate.** **SEN** These children should also play the game using centimetres. They should estimate the length, marking it out with the arrows, then measure. All to check measurements. Score accordingly (see Activity Sheet: Rules). **Supported.** **Key Vocabulary** **estimate, measure, accurate, accurately, length, centimetre, cm, millimetre, mm, metre, m, kilometre, km, to the nearest, standard unit of measurement**	Discuss the results of the game. ***How accurate were your estimates when you began the game?*** ***Did your accuracy improve as the game went on?*** ***What do you estimate the length of this object is, in mm?*** (Hold up a folder, book or similar.) Select a child to measure it. ***Who was within 10mm? 5mm? 2mm? 1cm?*** Repeat with other objects.

Measure Up Game

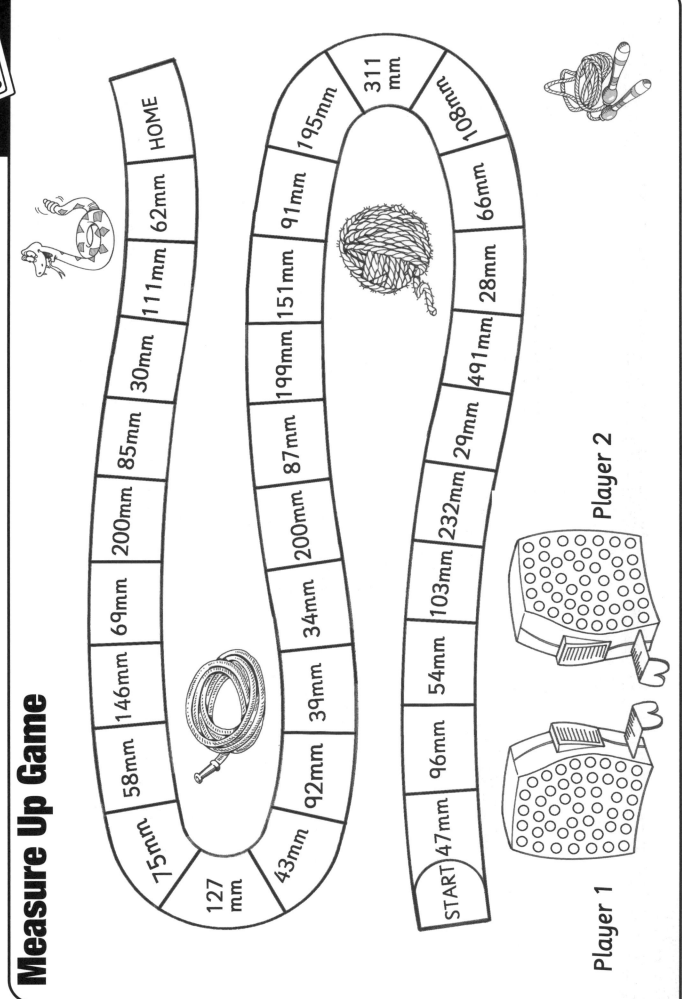

HOME | 62mm | 111mm | 30mm | 85mm | 200mm | 69mm | 146mm | 58mm | 75mm

127 mm | 43mm | 92mm | 39mm | 34mm | 200mm | 87mm | 199mm | 151mm | 91mm

195mm | 311 mm | 108mm | 66mm | 28mm | 491mm | 29mm | 232mm | 103mm | 54mm | 96mm | 47mm START

Player 1

Player 2

Sports Centre

Mental Starter

Learning Objective
- To multiply and divide by 10, 100 and 1000

What is an integer? A whole number.

On their individual whiteboards, after a count to ten, the children should show their answers to the following:

What is?…

53 x 10/100/1000
53 ÷ 10/100/1000
1.2 x 10/100/1000
1.2 ÷ 10/100/1000

Ask further questions randomly, using x and ÷ by 10, 100 and 1000.

Learning Objectives

- To solve one-step problems involving whole numbers and decimals
- To subtract mentally with integers and decimals in money notation

Success Criteria

- I can solve one-step problems involving whole numbers and decimals.
- I can subtract mentally with integers and decimals in money notation.

CD-ROM Resources

- PowerPoint file
- A3 copies of the Sports Centre Gameboard (Resource Sheet)
- Copies of the differentiated Activity Sheets

Other Resources

- Dice
- Counters
- Pencils
- Calculators

Introduction

Today we are going to play the Sports Centre Game, which involves subtracting.

How many pence in £1? 100p
How many pence in £10? 1,000p
How did you work it out? 100p x 10
So, how many pence in £100? 10,000p

Remind the children that it is often easier to convert £ & p to pence, carry out the calculation and then ÷ by 100 to convert it back.

How much is this in pence?
£3.95, £6.34, £19.99

How much is this in £s and pence?
416p, 987p, 109p

What is a running total? Demonstrate this for them.
You have a £50 budget. You spend £5.00 on an activity, so deduct it from the budget, leaving £45.00 (which is the running total). You spend another £3.50 on an activity, so deduct it from the running total, £45 and the new running total is £41.50.

Player 1	
£ spent	Amount left
£0.00	£50.00
£5.00	£45.00
£3.50	£41.50

What strategy can you use if you need to deduct (subtract) 99p?
Round up to 100p (£1), subtract and then add 1p.

Explain the activity. It is the summer holidays and you have a budget to spend on activities at the local sports centre.

The rules for the game are on the gameboard (Resource Sheet).

Activity

AA
These children should use their Activity Sheet to play the game with a total of £50 to spend. The prices include a range of digits in pence units.

MA
These children should use their Activity Sheet to play the game with a total of £50 to spend. The prices are in multiples of 5 or 10.

LA & SEN
These children should use their Activity Sheet to play the game with a total of £20 to spend. The prices are in multiples of 25, 50 or 75 with some whole £s.
Supported. Use money as an aid if appropriate.

NB: If this is too difficult for the LA children, play the game in a group using addition instead of subtraction.

Key Vocabulary

multiply, divide, integer, £, pounds, p, pence, decimal point, amount, money, running total, convert, mentally, subtraction, repeated subtraction, grand total, deduct

Plenary

How much change did you have left?

How many activities did you complete?

What strategies did you use to carry out the calculations?

Did anyone use a different strategy?

Select children from each group to share their strategies with the class.

Sports Centre Gameboard

Play with a partner, taking it in turns to go.

* Place your counters on the start.
* Player 1 throws the dice, moves that number of spaces, looks up the cost of the activity landed on and deducts the cost from the running total.
* Player 2 checks their answer on a calculator.
* Player 1 must deduct 50p from their running total if their calculation was incorrect!
* Player 2 then has their turn.
* If you land on a whistle, you have been told off for messing about, so you miss a go.
* If you land on a pair of trainers, you can race ahead two squares.
* The game ends when the first player reaches home or is asked to stop.
* The winner is the person who used their money to complete the most activities.

Mental Starter

Learning Objective
- To identify pairs of factors of 2-digit numbers

What is a factor? A number that multiplies with another one to make a third. For example, in 3 x 5 = 15 the factors are 3 and 5.

What is an integer? A whole number.

What are the integers in the sets of factors of:

12
(1 and 12, 2 and 6, 3 and 4)

24
(1 and 24, 2 and 12, 3 and 8, 4 and 6)

Repeat for other numbers.

Learning Objective
- To recognise that prime numbers have only two factors
- To identify prime numbers less than 100

Success Criteria
- I can recognise that prime numbers have only two factors.
- I can identify prime numbers less than 100.

CD-ROM Resources
- PowerPoint file
- Slide 6 in the PowerPoint file or an A3 copy of the Activity Sheet
- Slide 7 in the PowerPoint file or an A3 copy of Resource Sheet (Eratosthenes' Sieve rules)
- Copies of the differentiated Activity Sheets
- Slide 9 in the PowerPoint file or an A3 copy of the Answers Sheet

Other Resources
- Coloured pencils

Introduction

Today we are going to identify prime numbers less than 150 using Eratosthenes' Sieve.

What is the definition of a prime number? An integer that has only two integer factors, 1 and itself.

Explain that 1 is not a prime number because it only has one factor.

Can you tell me a prime number?
2, 3, 5, 7, 11, 13, 17, 19, 23 and so on.

Another?

Tell the children that you are going to tell them about Eratosthenes and his amazing work with prime numbers.

- Eratosthenes was a Greek mathematician.
- He lived from 275–194BCE.
- He was famous for his work on prime numbers.
- He invented a method of testing the first 100 numbers to see if they were prime numbers.
- He called it a sieve.
- It works in the same way as sieving flour.
- The lumps stay in the sieve, while the free-flowing flour does not. In this case, the prime numbers remain, while the others don't.

Display the Activity Sheet and the Resource Sheet. Explain the activity and demonstrate how to use the sieve.

Emphasise the importance of counting very carefully – one mistake will affect the whole pattern!

Activity

AA
These children should investigate prime numbers up to 200 using Eratosthenes' Sieve.
Extension: Continue the pattern to 250

MA
These children should investigate prime numbers up to 150 using Eratosthenes' Sieve.
Extension: Continue the pattern to 200

LA
These children should investigate prime numbers up to 100 using Eratosthenes' Sieve.
Support if appropriate.

SEN
These children should investigate prime numbers up to 50 using Eratosthenes' Sieve Support Sheet.
Supported.

NB: The completed sheet as it should look can be found in colour on the CD-ROM.

Key Vocabulary

prime number, number, factors, divisible, count on, multiples, integer, multiply, odd, even

Plenary

What are the prime numbers up to 50? 100? 150? 200?

Ask each ability group for the list of prime numbers they found in their activity and write them on the board.

Reinforce that even numbers can be divided by 1, itself and the number 2. This means that even numbers are not prime numbers except the number 2. The number 2 has only two factors, 1 and 2.

What two prime numbers added together make another prime number?
For example, 2 and 3.

Repeat the question several times, asking the children to use different prime numbers.

Display the Answers Sheet showing the coloured numbering of the prime numbers.

Prime Numbers

Eratosthenes' Sieve

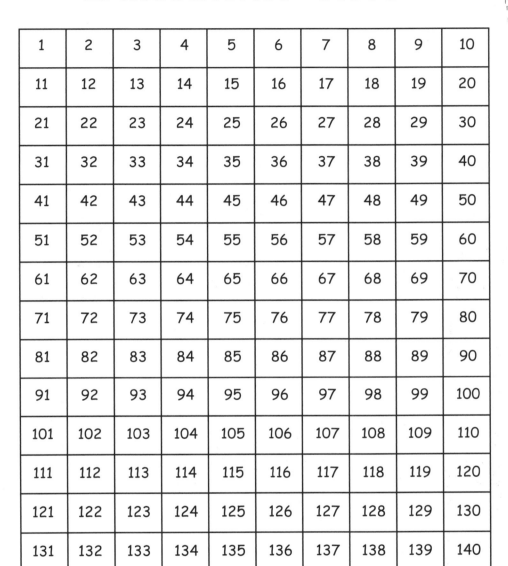

1	2	3	4	5	6	7	8	9	10
11	12	13	14	15	16	17	18	19	20
21	22	23	24	25	26	27	28	29	30
31	32	33	34	35	36	37	38	39	40
41	42	43	44	45	46	47	48	49	50
51	52	53	54	55	56	57	58	59	60
61	62	63	64	65	66	67	68	69	70
71	72	73	74	75	76	77	78	79	80
81	82	83	84	85	86	87	88	89	90
91	92	93	94	95	96	97	98	99	100
101	102	103	104	105	106	107	108	109	110
111	112	113	114	115	116	117	118	119	120
121	122	123	124	125	126	127	128	129	130
131	132	133	134	135	136	137	138	139	140
141	142	143	144	145	146	147	148	149	150

The prime numbers from 1-150 are: **2, 3, 5**

I can identify prime numbers less than 150. ☐

Mental Starter

Learning Objectives
- To consolidate use of inverse to make new number sentences

Can you make new number sentences from this one?

$25 \times 3 = 75$

$3 \times 25 = 75$
$75 \div 3 = 25$
$75 \div 25 = 3$
Repeat for several other sums.

Will the process change if I substitute a symbol for one of the numbers?

$\Omega \times 3 = 75$
$3 \times \Omega = 75$
$75 \div 3 = \Omega$
$75 \div \Omega = 3$

Write several sums on the board using a symbol. Ask the children to write number sentences for them.

How did you do it?

What strategies did you use?

Learning Objective

- To solve and make puzzles using symbols to represent numbers

Success Criteria

- I can solve and make puzzles using symbols to represent numbers.

CD-ROM Resources

- PowerPoint File
- Slides 5 and 6 in the PowerPoint file (Figures 1 and 2 on the Resource Sheet)
- Copies of the differentiated Activity Sheets
- Answers Sheet

Other Resources

- Scrap paper
- Pencils
- Rubbers

Introduction

Today we are going to solve puzzles using symbols to represent numbers and then make up our own puzzles.

Show Figure 1 on the Resource Sheet.
If ▱ + 4 = 10 what is the value of ▱?
⊠ × ⊠ = 64 what is the value of ⊠?
And so on. (See Answers Sheet for the answers.)

Remind children of the inverse.
If ☺ + ☺ + 9 = 17, then ☺ = 4. *Why?*
If $3 \times$ ▱ = 15, then ▱ = 5 *Why?*

Show Figure 2 on the Resource Sheet.
Can you work out the values of the symbols using the totals of the rows and columns?
How? What strategies can you use?

Explain that it is easier to begin with a row or column that has three of the same symbol. Point out that the second column along has three symbols the same.

Let's say ⅅ equals 10. Will that work?
Agree with the children that it does not work. Ask for suggestions for another number to try. (The answer is 8. See Answers Sheet.)

Once you have worked the values out, you then have two symbol values. Continue working this way so that you end up with all the values. (See Answers Sheet for all the answers.)

Explain the activity.

When they are ready to make up their own, advise them to:
- keep the symbols very simple;
- draw lightly in pencil so that they can alter them afterwards, when they are checking ;
- make sure they have one row or column with three symbols the same and several with two symbols the same in others.

Activity

AA 🁢

Independently, these children should complete the calculations to determine the value of the symbols. They then use these to determine which symbols are missing in the second puzzle grid. The symbols should be drawn in. The children should then make up their own puzzle using the one on the sheet as the format. (This can be done in pairs but recorded individually.) They should swap with a partner to check their puzzles work.

MA 🁢

Independently, these children must determine the value of each symbol using the total value of each row/column. They should then make up their own puzzles, using the first as the format. (This can be done in pairs.) They should swap with another pair to check that their puzzles work.

LA 🁢 **& SEN**

These children should work individually on the 3 x 3 grids. Each row and column must contain one of each symbol. They should fill in the missing symbols to complete the grid.

Extension: Move onto a simplified version of the 🁢 activity. Supported.

Key Vocabulary

number sentences, inverse, sum, total, row, column, symbol, puzzle, grid, value, multiplication, division

Plenary

Display the Answers Sheet for children to refer to over a period of time, so that they can check and understand.

Evaluate a puzzle from each ability group.

What strategies did you use?

What difficulties did you encounter?

How did you overcome them?

Does it work?

Could you improve it?

How?

Symbols Puzzles

✴ Complete this puzzle by finding the value of each symbol.

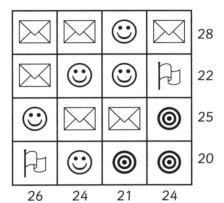

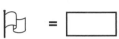

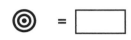

✴ Now make up some of your own puzzles.

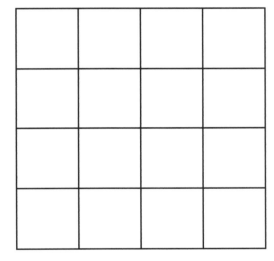

| | | | | | = | |

| | | | | | = | |

| | | | | | = | |

| | | | | | = | |

| | | | | | = | |

| | | | | | = | |

| | | | | | = | |

| | | | | | = | |

I can solve and make puzzles using symbols to represent numbers. ☐

Percentage Patterns

Mental Starter	Introduction	Activity	Plenary
Learning Objective • To revise what each digit represents in whole numbers and decimals with up to two places Write 15.62 on the board. **What does the 6 represent?** 6/10ths **What does the 2 represent?** 2/100ths **What does the 1 represent?** 10 Call out random numbers and ask: **What does this digit represent?** **LA & SEN** Ask the children to write: h t u . 1/10 1/100 on their whiteboards as a prompt.	*Today we are going to focus on percentages.* Explain to the children that 1% is 1/100. Display the coloured grid (Resource Sheet) or the multi-link 10 x 10 square. *This is a 10 x 10 square, so how many squares/cubes altogether?* Explain that the whole square is 100% (100 squares), and each small square or cube is 1%. *How many small squares/cubes are red? blue? and so on.* List each colour and the number of those small squares/cubes on the board. As a whole class, add the totals together, making 100. Emphasise that the small squares/cubes can be anywhere in the square. They are still 1% each. *What fraction is each cube?* 1/100th *What percentage is that?* 1% *What fraction is 10 cubes?* 10/100 or 1/10 *What percentage is that?* 10% *What percentage is* 1/4? 25/100 or 25% *And* 1/2? 50/100 or 50% *And* 3/4? 75/100 or 75% Explain the activity.	**AA** These children should make up their own percentage patterns on the 10 x 10 grids on the Activity Sheet, listing the colours, percentages and decimal fractions and totalling them to make 100%. They should swap with a partner to check their answers. **MA** These children should make up their own percentage patterns on the 10 x 10 grids on the Activity Sheet, listing the colours and percentages, and totalling them to make 100%. They should swap with partner and check their answers. **LA & SEN** These children should make up own percentage patterns on the first 10 x 10 square on the Activity Sheet, showing 25% in one colour, 75% in another. They then repeat this for 50%. **Support as required.** **NB:** Tell the children that if the total of each percent is not 100 then they must check and alter their colour totals.	Show the class some of the MA and AA patterns. Check the totals of the colours. *Can you put crosses randomly in the 10 x 10 grid in green to represent 35%?* *... and in blue to represent 7/100?* Repeat with other similar questions, asking fractions of the AA group and percentages of the other two ability groups.

Learning Objective
• To understand percentages as the number of parts in every 100

Success Criteria
• I can understand percentages as the number of parts in every 100.

CD-ROM Resources
• PowerPoint file
• Slide 4 in the PowerPoint file (coloured grid)
• Two A3 10 x 10 blank grids
• Printed copy of the coloured grid (Resource Sheet) or a prepared 10 x 10 grid using randomly coloured multi-link cubes
• Copies of the differentiated Activity Sheets

Other Resources
• Whiteboards and pens
• Coloured markers
• Squared paper
• Coloured pencils
• Rulers

Key Vocabulary
decimals, fractions, units, tens, hundreds, decimal point, tenths, hundredths, percent, percentages, %, total

Percentage Patterns

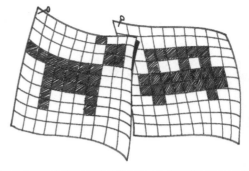

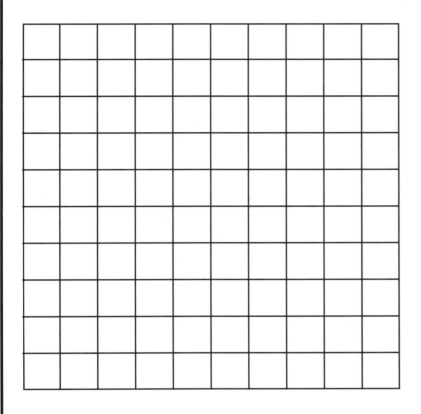

Colour	Percentage
	%
	%
	%
	%
	%
	%
Total	%

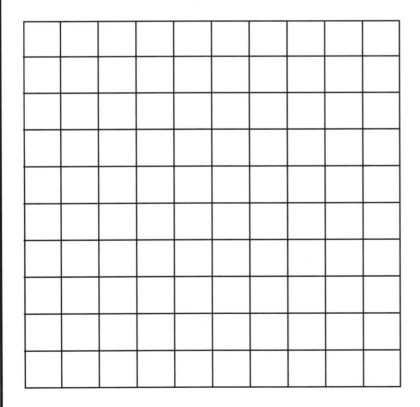

Colour	Percentage
	%
	%
	%
	%
	%
	%
Total	%

I can find the percentage of each colour in my pattern, totalling 100%. ☐

Clock This!

Mental Starter	Learning Objective	Introduction	Activity	Plenary
Learning Objective	• To solve problems involving 24-hour clock notation	***Today we are going to play a game involving the 24-hour clock.***	The answers (Answers Sheet) should be on the teacher's desk for children to go and check when necessary.	Play 24-hour bingo.
• To reinforce facts connected with time		***When using the 24-hour clock, how do we know when a time is am?***		The children draw a 3 x 3 grid on their individual whiteboards.
How many seasons are there in a year?	**Success Criteria**	We add a 0 to the time if it is a single digit, such as 09:00.	**AA**	Ask them to write in random times (hours) in 24-hour notation.
	• I can solve problems using 24-hour clock notation.	***What is 12 midnight on the 24-hour clock?*** 00.00	Give the children a copy of the rules (Resource Sheet 2) as well as the relevant Activity Sheet. They should write their answers in their books or on paper. Answers are to be labelled according to the question numbers. The children should play the game in pairs, giving answers to the two questions corresponding to each number landed on. Both answers have to be correct to score.	
What are they?		***What is midday?*** 12.00		Call out times in 12-hour form, using am and pm.
	CD-ROM Resources	Reinforce that am is up to 12 o'clock (noon) and after that it is pm, and that 12 o'clock midnight is 00:00. 1 minute past is 00:01. 1 hour past is 01:00. 1pm after 12 o'clock (noon) = 13:00, 2pm = 14:00 and so on.		The children convert and cross out the time if it matches one in their grid.
How many months are there in a year? What are they?	• PowerPoint file	Show the 24-hour clock on the gameboard as a prompt.	**MA**	
Remind the children of the rhyme '30 days has September….'	• Copies of the gameboard (Resource Sheet 1)		Give the children a copy of the rules (Resource Sheet 2) as well as the relevant Activity Sheet. They should write their answers in their books or on paper. Answers are to be labelled according to the question numbers. The should children play the game in pairs, giving an answer to the question corresponding to each number landed on.	
	• Copies of the rules (Resource Sheet 2)	***What time is 7pm on the 24-hour clock?***		
How many weeks in a year?	• Answers Sheet	Repeat for other times.		
	• Copies of the differentiated Activity Sheets	***Who has a strategy for converting from 12 to 24 and back?***	**LA & SEN**	
How many days in a year?		Paired talk, then share with the whole class.	Give the children a copy of the rules (Resource Sheet 2) as well as the relevant Activity Sheet. The children should play the game, converting times to the 12-hour clock from the 24-hour clock and vice versa, corresponding to the number landed on. Answers are to be written on the Activity Sheet. **With support.**	
How many hours in a day? How many of them are night time? How many are daytime?	**Other Resources**	Explain that GMT is Greenwich Mean Time (British Time). BST is British Summer Time. In the spring we put our clocks forward by an hour. In the autumn we revert back to GMT by putting our clocks back by an hour. We do this so that it is lighter in the mornings in winter for children to walk to school and for the farmers to be able to see to do jobs such as milking the cows.		
	• A 24-hour analogue clock to demonstrate		**Key Vocabulary**	
How many minutes in an hour?	• Paper or maths books for answers to be written on	Discuss strategies for choosing the correct operation to answer certain questions. For example, if you are given the arrival time and length of a flight, what operation would you need to find the departure time? Bear in mind local time (+ or –).	**day, week, month, year, season, time, 24 hours, 12 hours, day, night, midday, midnight, noon, am, pm, clock, o'clock, hours, minutes, seconds**	
How many seconds in a minute?	• Red and green pencil	Explain the activity.		
	• Dice			
	• Different coloured counters			
	• Whiteboards and pens			

Clock This!

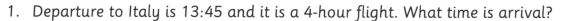

❋ **All times are GMT unless you are asked for local time.**

1. Departure to Italy is 13:45 and it is a 4-hour flight. What time is arrival?

2. Departure to Israel is 16:40 and arrival is 23:20. How long is the flight?

3. Departure to Russia is 09:25 and arrival is 11:30. How long is the flight?

4. Arrival at Dubai, United Arab Emirates is at 6.30am. The flight is 7 hours 5 minutes. What time is departure?

5. Departure to Salt Lake City, USA is 05:20 and arrival is 21:50. How long is the flight?

6. Departure to Singapore is 12:00. It is a 13-hour flight. What time is arrival?

7. Arrival at Portugal is 10:05. The flight is 2 hours 55 minutes. What time is departure?

8. Arrival from Majorca is 23:50. What time was the departure for the 2½-hour flight?

9. Departure from Greece to London is 16:45 (local time) and Greece is 3 hours ahead of GMT. What is the departure time in GMT?

10. The flight to Marrakesh, Morocco departing at 23:30 is overbooked. The next flight is 2½ hours later. What time is departure?

11. Departure from Accra, Ghana to London is 03:00. It is a 7-hour flight. What time is arrival?

12. Arrival at Kiev, Ukraine is 02:20 and departure was 23:00. How long is the flight?

13. The flight to Vancouver, Canada is 10 hours 5 minutes. If departure is at 21:30, what time is arrival?

14. Turkey is 3 hours ahead. If departure was 17:55 GMT, what was it in local time?

15. The flight to Vilnius, Lithuania is 3 hours. What time was departure if arrival was 08:50?

16. Departure to Dubai is 17:40 and arrival is 00:45. How long is the flight?

17. Departure to the Netherlands is 13:55 and the flight takes 1 hour 10 minutes. What time is arrival?

18. Departure to Spain is 14:25 and it is a 2½-hour flight. Spain is 1 hour ahead. What time is arrival local time?

19. You are flying to Australia but have to stop over in Hong Kong for two hours to refuel. London to Hong Kong is 12 hours 50 minutes and Hong Kong to Australia is 8 hours 50 minutes. How many hours will you be travelling, including stopover time?

20. Arrival at Cancun, Mexico is 11 hours after departure, which is 12:20. What time is arrival?

21. London to Sydney takes 23½ hours. If arrival is at 9:30am, what time is departure?

22. Arrival at Bratislava is 11:50pm and departure is 8.30pm. How long is the flight?

23. Two planes land, one at 9:30pm and one at 19:30. Which is the earlier time?

00. Congratulations, you have completed the game!

I can solve problems using the 24-hour clock notation. ☐

Call My Bluff

Learning Objectives	Introduction	Activity	Plenary
• To introduce new vocabulary • To practise using a dictionary	***Today we are going to play a vocabulary game, 'Call My Bluff'.*** ***You will be introduced to new words, each with three possible definitions (meanings). Only one of the definitions is true, the other two are bluffs.***	**In mixed ability pairs within two teams, as set up in Introduction.** The pairs within the two teams have been given their words and definitions and found the correct one. As they play the game, each pair will read out their word and definitions to the opposing team and that team's allocated pair must guess which is the correct definition.	***What new words have you learned today?*** ***What are their meanings/definitions?***
Success Criteria	***How do we use a dictionary to find the meaning of a new word?*** Choose some children to explain to the class. Briefly run through the rules for using a dictionary.	• Someone from Team A reads out their word, giving the correct pronunciation, and all three definitions.	***Which is your favourite?*** The children should evaluate the new words the class found, choose a favourite and explain why they like it. Because of the way it sounds? The way it looks? Its meaning?
• I can learn new vocabulary. • I can practise using a dictionary.	Make sure the children know what is meant by 'bluffing'.	• The first pair in Team B confer and then agree which definition they believe to be true.	
	Explain that the class will be split into two teams and the children will work in pairs within their teams. (They should be working in mixed ability teams and pairs.) In preparation for the game, give each pair one or two word cards. Explain that they must look the word up in a dictionary to find the correct definition out of the three given on the card. They should tick that definition.	• Team A confirms this is correct or incorrect by holding up the correct TRUE or BLUFF card. • Someone from Team A then reads out the definition of the word. • Team B's first pair then has their first word and definitions shown and Team A's first pair guesses.	***Were the words unusual?*** ***Was it easy to guess the real meanings/definitions?*** ***What else do we use a dictionary for?***
CD-ROM Resources			
• PowerPoint file • 'Call My Bluff' cards, cut up into individual word cards for each team (Resource Sheets 1–3) • Copy of Answers Sheet	Ensure the children are given correct pronunciation before moving on to the next word! If some pairs finish this task early, they can help other pairs in their team who haven't. Each pair should also prepare a TRUE card and a BLUFF card.	**Scoring** The teacher is game host and score-keeper. One point should be awarded for each correct guess. The team with the highest total wins.	
Other Resources	Make sure the children understand that, while they will know the true meaning of the word, their opposing team must not know as when the game is played, they have to guess the correct definition.		
• Dictionaries and/or online dictionaries • Pencils • Paper and marker pens for making the True/Bluff cards	**Additional activity** This activity can be extended by asking the children, in mixed ability groups, to look up new, interesting and unusual words and writing three definitions for them, as in the game. One definition must be correct. Encourage them to be imaginative in their 'bluff' definitions, using the word's spelling or sound as clues to a possible bluff; for example, 'remorse' – Inspector Morse, Morse code. Provide A5 pieces of blank paper for them to write their clues on, reminding them to write the letter for the correct definition lightly on the back (so it doesn't show through).	**Key Vocabulary** **vocabulary, words, dictionary, definition, meaning, spelling, pronounce, pronunciation**	

Call My Bluff

Team A words

syntax
a) tax collector from the Roman times
b) putty for sticking things
c) the way words are arranged

confer
a) have a discussion
b) type of evergreen tree
c) fruit from a horse-chestnut tree

monocle
a) a lens worn over one eye
b) an overhead railway in Japan
c) a design made up of letters

clamour
a) a loud, confused noise
b) a mix between a cleaver and a hammer
c) to climb with difficulty

brier
a) a thorny bush
b) someone who buys something
c) someone who brings things

Team B words

poise
a) pointing your toes
b) to stop for a minute
c) balance

hypocrite
a) eating too much sugar
b) someone who goes against their word
c) a place in Greece

lorgnette
a) a group of long nettles
b) a pair of spectacles held on a long handle
c) underwear for ladies

pict
a) a member of an ancient tribe of Scotland
b) to pick someone out
c) a type of weapon

lepidopterous
a) a type of dinosaur
b) a type of butterfly or moth
c) an animal that lives in the desert

Start a Sentence

Learning Objective	Introduction	Activity	Plenary

Learning Objective
- To use connectives in writing

Success Criteria
- I can use connectives in my writing.

CD-ROM Resources
- PowerPoint file
- Slide 7 in the PowerPoint file or an A3 copy of the gameboard (Resource Sheet 1) to demonstrate how the game can be played
- Copy of the gameboard for each group (Resource Sheet 1)
- Copy of the rules (Resource Sheet 2)

Other Resources
- Dice
- Counters
- Sheets of lined paper
- Pencils

Introduction

Today we are going to revise connectives and play a connectives game.

What is a connective?
A connective is a word or phrase that links clauses or sentences. It can be a *conjunction* (like *but, when, and, because*) or an *adverb* (like *however, then, therefore*). Connectives help to make the different parts of a text fit together logically.

What are the different uses of connectives?
Discuss the following with the class:
addition – also, furthermore, moreover
opposition – however, nevertheless, on the other hand
reinforcing – besides, anyway, after all
explaining – for example, in other words, that is to say
listing – firstly, first of all, finally
indicating result – therefore, consequently, as a result
indicating time – just then, meanwhile, later.

Explain that today they will be concentrating on connectives that can begin a sentence.

Which connectives can begin a sentence?
Write some on the board. (You can choose from the list above.) Then explain that you are going to begin writing a story using a connective to begin each sentence. Model the sentence below (or one that you have made up).

Eventually, the haggard, sad, old tramp began to rise up from the gnarled bench, almost in slow motion, his damp bones creaking with age and fatigue.

Now, can anyone give me a sentence beginning with a connective that continues the story I've begun?
Write some on the board. Repeat this with other sentences.

Explain that the object of the game they will be playing is to continue this story using sentences that begin with the connectives landed on. Show the children the gameboard (Resource Sheet 1) and explain the rules. Remind them to use a dictionary if they are unsure of the meaning of any word.

Activity

In mixed ability groups
- Using connectives generated by the gameboard on Resource Sheet 1, each group should continue the story that was started in the Introduction. The children take it in turns, using the connective they land on to make a sentence. (See the rules below. A larger version of the rules for display is on Resource Sheet 2.)
- The sentences must carry on from each other to continue the story.
- Every member of each group must take a turn to write a sentence.
- Higher ability children may support lower ability children.
- If necessary, a group may elect a scribe from the more able children.

The rules of the game
- Place the counter on START.
- Take it in turns to throw the dice and move that number of spaces, following the direction of the arrows. Move round the outside track clockwise and the inner track anti-clockwise.
- Write a descriptive sentence beginning with the word or words you land on, being careful to continue the group's story.
- Don't forget: check each sentence for sense, punctuation, powerful verbs, adjectives and adverbs.
- The game ends when either you reach the word STOP, or you are asked to stop by the teacher.

Key Vocabulary

connectives, clauses, sequence of events, addition, opposition, reinforcing, explaining, listing, indicating result/time, sentences, descriptive language

Plenary

Share the groups' stories with the class.

Have they used the connectives in the correct context?

Do their sentences continue the story?

Have they used descriptive language?

How could you improve it?

Remind the children to use connectives in their writing as much as possible to make it more interesting for the audience.

Start a Sentence

Because

At first

As long as

Just then

Then

When

Before

If   Next

At last

Besides

Instead

Eventually

Unless

Finally

Since

Whenever

After

START ↑

STOP

Meanwhile Whenever

As long as →

↓

Suddenly

While

Later

Although

In due course

Until

So

Once

Until

Though

By this time

In spite of

As a result

The next day

Colour Metaphors

	Introduction	Activity	Plenary
Learning Objective • To describe colours using metaphors	***Today we are going to use adjectives to write some metaphors.*** Read your favourite metaphor poem that contains a description of colour or read out the poem 'Grey' (Resource Sheet 1). ***What is a metaphor?*** It is language that describes something as if it is something else, using the words 'is' or 'are'. It paints a picture with words. For example: *The sun is a yellow flower holding its head up high.* *Clouds are white balls of cotton wool.* ***What is the difference between a metaphor and a simile?*** Instead of saying something 'is' something else, a simile uses the word 'like' or 'as'. For example: *The sun is like a red ball.* Give the children a copy of the poem. Reread it, asking them to listen carefully and follow the text. Allow them three minutes to highlight all the metaphors, such as 'Grey is the sky'. Discuss the poem and the fact that they may have highlighted the whole of it. It is, in fact, a poem made up of metaphors. ***Does the metaphor make you 'see it' in your mind?*** Model writing some metaphors using other colours, emphasising the importance of using strong descriptive words and phrases to paint a picture in the reader's mind. For example, 'Red is the droplet of blood on my grazed knee'. Write another colour on the board. ***Think of a metaphor to describe that colour.*** Select some children to share their ideas. Ask the class to evaluate the ideas. ***Did the words paint a picture? How could s/he improve it?*** Explain how to play the game and ensure that the children can read the colours and know what they are.	**AA** 🎲 In pairs, the children play the game. They should individually write a metaphor for each colour landed on, and then rewrite it as a simile. They should write at least four metaphors and similes each. **MA** 🎲 In pairs, the children play the game, individually writing metaphors. They should write at least four metaphors each. **LA** 🎲 **& SEN** As a group, the children play the game on an enlarged board, taking it in turns and making up metaphors that an adult can scribe. More able children can use a whiteboard with the adult helping them to scribe if necessary. They could then copy the completed metaphor into their book or onto paper. **Support as appropriate.** **The rules of the game** • Place the counters on START. • Children take turns to throw the dice and move across board. • They write a metaphor using the colour landed on. • While the first child is writing their metaphor, the second takes their turn. • Continue until HOME is reached. • If there is sufficient time, play again.	Discuss and evaluate some of the metaphors the children have made up. ***Who can write a metaphor for a shape?*** Select children from different ability groups to suggest different metaphors for a range of different two- and three-dimensional shapes. Write them on the board. ***Does this metaphor make you 'see it' in your mind – does it paint a picture with the words?***
Success Criteria • I can describe colours using metaphors.			
CD-ROM Resources • PowerPoint file • Slide 8 in the PowerPoint file or an A3 copy of the Colour Metaphors gameboard (Resource Sheet 2) to demonstrate how the game can be played • Copies of Resource Sheets 1 and 2 • For **LA/SEN:** one A3 copy of Resource Sheet 2			
Other Resources • Highlighters or coloured pencils • Dice • Counters • Pens • Literacy books or lined paper		**Key Vocabulary** **metaphor, simile, descriptive, adjectives, adverbs, phrases, describe, imaginative**	

Colour Metaphors Game

Rules

- Work with a partner.
- Place your counters on START.
- Take turns to throw the dice and move across the board the same number of spaces as the number thrown.
- Write a metaphor using the colour landed on. (Remember to 'paint a picture' with your words.)
- While your partner is writing their metaphor, you can take your turn.
- Continue till you reach HOME.
- If there is sufficient time, play again.

HOME tangerine copper navy turquoise lemon indigo peach

white lime fuchsia bronze orange cream violet

maroon red grey green beige cerise brown yellow aqua

gold purple silver black blue pink START

Silly Sentences

Learning Objectives

- To consolidate knowledge of word classes
- To identify and use all word classes in alliterative sentences

Success Criteria

- I can identify and use all word classes in alliterative sentences.

CD-ROM Resources

- PowerPoint file
- Copies of the Activity Sheet for the LA/SEN children

Other Resources

- Pens
- Literacy books
- Dictionaries

Introduction

Today we are going to be word-class detectives. Using what we already know, we are going to find some word classes in sentences. After that we will use set word classes to write silly sentences.

What job does a noun do? Names a person, place, thing or idea.

Can you give me an example?

Write examples on board.

Repeat for:

- adjective (describes somebody or something)
- verb (expresses an action or state of being)
- adverb (describes a verb, adjective or another adverb)

Tell the children that adjectives and adverbs help to paint a picture with words. Then write this sentence on the board: *The old tramp slept awkwardly.*

Can you identify the noun/verb/adjective/adverb in this sentence?

Write the appropriate abbreviation above each word as it is identified.

	adj.	n.	v.	adv.
	The	old	tramp	slept	awkwardly.

Explain that adverbs are not always right next to the verb. You have to find the adverb and hunt for the matching verb.

What is alliteration?

Explain that the activity they are about to do is to use alliteration and find an adjective, noun, verb and adverb all beginning with the same phoneme; for example, *Slimy snakes slither slowly, Cautious cats creep carefully* and *Awful Arthur ate atrociously.*

Remind the children to find alternative words in a dictionary and to edit their work to ensure that their grammar is correct.

Activity

The children are free to choose whether they wish to select their own letters to use for the activity or use the letters of their names.

AA

Individually, these children should produce sentences using alliteration and containing all the word classes in the correct order: adjective, noun, verb, adverb. These sentences can be recorded in their literacy books. These children should be able to complete at least eight sentences.

MA

In pairs, these children should produce sentences using alliteration and containing all the word classes in the correct order: adjective, noun, verb, adverb. Each pair should be able to complete at least five sentences.

LA & SEN

With support and an adult scribing, these children should produce word banks using alliteration (see the Activity Sheet). Copy and stick their finished work into their books.

Key Vocabulary

word classes, noun, adjective, verb, adverb, sentence, alliteration, grammar, powerful language, descriptive, dictionary

Plenary

Share some sentences from the AA and MA groups.

Evaluate them as a class.

Have they used the correct word classes?

Select some words from the LA/SEN groups and put them together as sentences on the board.

Silly Sentences Word Bank

Adjective	Noun (plural)	Verb	Adverb
Silly	snakes	slither	slowly
Cautious	cats	creep	carefully

☐ I can make a word bank for all word classes, using alliteration.

The Sound Collector

Learning Objective

- To write a new poem based upon one we read

Success Criteria

- I can write a new poem based upon one we read.

CD-ROM Resources

- PowerPoint file
- Slide 3 in the PowerPoint file or an enlarged copy of the Resource Sheet
- Copies of the Resource Sheet
- Copies of the Activity Sheet for LA and SEN children

Other Resources

- Glue
- Literacy books or lined paper
- Whiteboards and pens
- Pens
- Rhyming dictionaries
- Thesauruses

Introduction

Today we are going to write a poem based on one we will read.

Give the children a copy of the poem 'The Sound Collector' (Resource Sheet) and read it with them as a shared reading session.

What is the poem about? An unknown person who collects all the household sounds, leaving it in silence.

What is the pattern of the poem?

- Each verse is four lines.
- The rhyming pattern is A B C B.
- The rhythm is regular.
- The first and last verses share the same first line.
- Most lines of the other verses contain an onomatopoeic verb and a noun; for example, *The ticking of the clock.*
- Some of the ideas are spread over two lines.
- There is no punctuation except for a full stop at the end of first and last verses.

What is onomatopoeia? (A word that sounds like the noise it describes, such as 'crash' and 'tinkle')

Give the children three minutes to highlight all the onomatopoeic words in the poem.

Look at the rhythm and clap it out with the class.

Model writing another verse on the board:

The flushing of the toilet
The flicking of the switch
The booting of the ball
Across the football pitch

Is the rhythm correct?
Have I kept to the A B C B pattern?
What onomatopoeic verbs can you think of?

Explain the activity. Stress that sometimes a line just won't work and you have to start again. Encourage the use of thesauruses and rhyming dictionaries.

Activity

AA

These children should stick the highlighted poem into their books. Then, individually, they should write the first verse on the next page. They then write their own version of the poem, using whiteboards so that they can edit them until they are happy with the pattern and rhythm. They then write their edited version in their books after the first verse and write the last verse of the original.

MA

These children should work in pairs, collaborating with ideas, while writing in their own books. They should stick the highlighted poem into their books and then write the first verse on the next page. They then write their own version of the poem, using whiteboards so that they can edit them until they are happy with the pattern and rhythm. They then write their edited version in their books after the first verse and write the last verse of the original.

LA & SEN

Those children who are able could write their own version of the poem using the first and last verse and writing two verses in the scaffold (Activity Sheet). Those who are not able may write non-rhyming verses and work in a group. **Support should be given where appropriate.**

Key Vocabulary

poem, line, verse, rhyme, rhyme pattern, onomatopoeia, onomatopoeic, verb, rhythm, punctuation

Plenary

Select one or two children from each ability group to share their poems with the class.

Ask the class to evaluate them:

Was the rhythm correct?

Did it keep to the A B C B pattern?

Were the verbs onomatopoeic?

Return to the original poem again and ask the children to think of sound effects for it. Read the poem aloud with the children contributing their sound effects.

The Sound Collector

A stranger called this morning
Dressed all in black and grey
Put every sound into a bag
And carried them away.

The whistling of the kettle
The turning of the lock
The purring of the kitten
The ticking of the clock

The popping of the toaster
The crunching of the flakes
When you spread the marmalade
The scraping noise it makes

The hissing of the frying-pan
The ticking of the grill
The bubbling of the bathtub
As it starts to fill

The drumming of the raindrops
On the window-pane
When you do the washing-up
The gurgle of the drain

The crying of the baby
The squeaking of the chair
The swishing of the curtain
The creaking of the stair

A stranger called this morning
He didn't leave his name
Left us only silence
Life will never be the same.

ROGER MCGOUGH

Dictionary Challenge

Learning Objective

- To practise dictionary skills

Success Criteria

- I can practise my dictionary skills by completing a quiz.

CD-ROM Resources

- PowerPoint file
- Slide 4 in the PowerPoint file or an enlarged copy of the top part of the Resource Sheet
- Slide 5 in the PowerPoint file or an enlarged copy of the Resource Sheet
- Copies of the Resource Sheet
- Copies of the differentiated Activity Sheets
- Slide 8 in the PowerPoint file or an enlarged copy of the Activity Sheet

Other Resources

- Dictionaries
- Lined paper
- Pencils

Introduction

Today we are going to revise how to use a dictionary and then complete a quiz.

How are words listed in a dictionary? Alphabetically.

What other use does a dictionary have apart from checking the spelling of a word? Finding the definition (meaning).

Often the dictionary will tell you what word class a word is. What is a word class? Noun, adjective, verb, adverb.
Explain that sometimes it will even tell you how to pronounce the word and its origin (where it comes from).

Using the dictionary page (Resource Sheet), discuss how the page is laid out.

What is a guide word? The first word on the page is shown at the top left of each page and the last word listed on the page is shown on the top right, for quick reference.

Tell the children that they are going to look for the word 'school'.

So to find 'school', what do we look for first?
- First we find 's' in the dictionary.
- Next we look at the next letter in the word, 'c'.
- Now we look at the third letter in the word, 'h'.
We keep doing this until we have found the correct word.

NB. When looking up words in the dictionary as a whole-class activity, be aware that different ability groups may be using different dictionaries, so you may need to elicit three different answers to each question.

Now, working in pairs, look up the word 'flame' in the dictionary. What page number is it on?
How many different meanings does it give? What are they? Does it give a word class? What is it?

Repeat this for the word 'heal'.
Explain the activity.

Activity

AA
In pairs, these children should complete Parts 1 and 2 of Activity Sheet , writing the answers on a sheet of lined paper.
Extension: Challenge this group to write a definition of the word 'box', first in four words, then three, then two and finally one word. Repeat this for 'pen'.

MA
In pairs, these children should complete Part 1 of Activity Sheet , writing the answers on a sheet of lined paper.
Extension: Challenge this group to open their dictionary to any page. What is the longest/shortest word on the page? What do the words mean?

LA & SEN
The children should complete Activity Sheet as a group with support.

Key Vocabulary

dictionary, alphabetical, alphabetically, spelling, word class, noun, n, adjective, adj, verb, v, adverb, adv, definition, guide word, pronunciation, pronounce

Plenary

How do we look up words in the dictionary?

Display and work through the Activity Sheet with the whole class, writing the answers on the board, so that the LA/SEN group can feed back.

Ask for a volunteer from the AA group to challenge the class with one of their made-up questions.

Dictionary Challenge

✳ Use a dictionary to complete these challenges.

✳ Write the answers on a sheet of paper, making sure you label them carefully.

Part 1

a) Find four words that begin with 'gh'. Write them down and give the pages you found them on.

b) Find four words that begin with 'pri'. Write them down and give the pages you found them on.

c) Find two words that begin with 'plea'. Write them down and give the pages you found them on.

d) List some words that sound like they begin with an 'n' but actually begin with a 'k'. Write the pages you found them on.

e) Find a word that begins with a double letter. Write it down and give the page you found it on.

f) How many different meanings are listed for the word 'stable'?

g) Find six words that have only two letters. Write them down and give the pages you found them on.

h) Find the word 'piano'. What are the guide words on the page that you found them?

i) Write a definition of the word 'car' first in 4 words, then 3, then 2 and finally 1 word.

Part 2

Write three more dictionary questions and challenge your partner to find the answers.

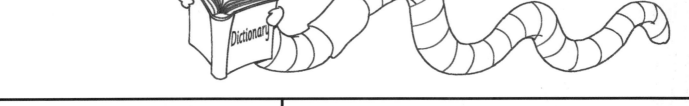

I can practise my dictionary skills. ☐

Complex Carousel

Learning Objective
- To secure knowledge of complex sentences by changing simple sentences into complex ones

Success Criteria
- I can change simple sentences into complex ones.

CD-ROM Resources
- PowerPoint file
- Copies of the Resource Sheet – cut up (one for each table)

Other Resources
- Lined paper
- Pens

Introduction

Today we are going to practise complex sentences by playing a game.

What is a complex sentence? One that has a main clause and a subordinate clause.

What is a main clause? A simple sentence, such as *The cat sat on the mat.*

What is a subordinate clause? A part of a sentence that doesn't make sense on its own and is dependent on the main clause. It can be an adjectival, adverbial or noun phrase. For example: *The cat, who was exhausted, sat on the mat.*

Explain that the phrase can be in the middle, beginning or end of the sentence. For example:
The cat sat on the mat because it was exhausted.
Because it was exhausted, the cat sat on the mat.
The cat, because it was exhausted, sat on the mat.

Introduce the idea that complex sentences can use connectives – especially 'who', 'whose', 'which' and 'that' – and powerful or strong verbs in the gerund (-ing form).
The tree, which stood in the garden, was green.
Charlie Chaplin, who was a famous actor, appeared in many silent movies.
Although the sun was shining, I was still feeling chilly.
Shuffling across the room, the naughty boy grinned.

Point out the use of commas.

Write some simple sentences on the board. (*The fish swam in the bowl. The leaves were falling.*)

Can you change each simple sentence into a complex sentence?

Select children to come up and write them on the board.

Explain the activity.

Activity

In ability groups

The children should work individually, within their ability groups.

1. Give each child a piece of lined paper and a pen.

2. They should write a very simple sentence (main clause) or select one from the centre of the table (see CD-ROM Resources).

3. When the teacher says 'Go', they should pass their sheet to the person sitting next to them in their group, clockwise.

4. On receipt of the sheet, each child should rewrite the original sentence as a complex one, underneath the original.

5. The sheet is passed to the next child, clockwise, and the whole process repeated.

LA & SEN
Support as appropriate.

Key Vocabulary

sentence, simple, complex, main clause, subordinate clause, phrase, connectives, strong verb, adverbial phrase, adjectival phrase, noun phrase, descriptive, gerund

Plenary

Who can tell me what a complex sentence is?

Who can tell me what a main clause is?

Who can tell me what a subordinate clause is?

Ask children from each group to come up and read out or write on the board one of their simple sentences made into a complex one.

Write a simple sentence on the board, such as *The child sat in the chair.*

Who can make this into a complex sentence using an adverbial phrase/adjectival phrase?

Explain to the children that now that they know how to write complex sentences it is important to use them in their writing.

Remind them, however, that using very short sentences occasionally, adds to the drama and urgency of their writing.

Complex Carousel

Lee ate his dinner.

The class was excited.

The cat was frightened.

Cerys turned on the computer.

The game was interesting.

The flower was purple.

The dog howled.

The girl danced.

The girl sat on the bench.

The teacher was astounded.

Jordan was excited.

The book had many pages.

Perfect Punctuation

Learning Objectives

- To punctuate sentences accurately, including speech marks
- To use punctuation to clarify meaning in complex sentences

Success Criteria

- I can punctuate sentences accurately.

CD-ROM Resources

- PowerPoint file
- Slide 6 in the PowerPoint file or an enlarged copy of Resource Sheet 1
- A copy of Resource Sheet 2 for reference
- Copies of the differentiated Activity Sheets
- Copy of the Answers Sheet for reference

Other Resources

- Pens
- Literacy books or lined paper
- Glue

Introduction

Today we are going to practise our punctuation skills.

When do we use a capital letter? At the beginning of a sentence and also for proper nouns (names).

When do we use a full stop? At the end of a sentence.

What other punctuation marks can we use at the end of a sentence? Exclamation mark, question mark.

What do we use apostrophes for? Contraction (don't) and possession (Laura's). Remind the children that an apostrophe is not used when making words plural. This a common mistake when looking at apostrophes for possession. (tomatoe's)

How do we punctuate speech? Use opening speech marks prior to speaking. Use a comma, question or exclamation mark immediately after the speech. Then use closing speech marks. Emphasise that this is only around words that are actually spoken, not reported speech, such as 'She said she was ….'

What do we use commas for? In between items in a list; to make sense within complex sentences, especially to separate adjectival and adverbial phrases; to indicate a pause for breath.

Display the 'Dusty The Hamster' text (Resource Sheet 1) and explain that you were in a hurry to type this and forgot the punctuation marks. Read a bit of the text without inflection in your voice and without stopping at the end of a sentence, as a graphic example of why we need punctuation.

Invite the children to add the missing punctuation (in the order in which it is required) on the board or on the A3 copy. Discuss any issues as they arise, asking them why they have done that. (A punctuated version may be found on Resource Sheet 2.)

Emphasise to the children that we should all be using this punctuation whenever we write.

Explain the activity.

Activity

All the children's work should be written in their literacy books or on lined paper. It should be named (if on paper), dated and the relevant learning objective written as the title.

AA 🎴

Individually, these children should read the passage carefully, determining where the sentences begin and end. They should then rewrite the passage, a sentence at a time, using punctuation accurately. **NB:** Kiera's explanation contains speech within speech, so should be punctuated with single quote marks within double quote marks. See Answers Sheet.

Extension: They could write some complex sentences of their own, punctuating them correctly.

MA 🎴

Working in pairs, one child reads the first sentence aloud to their partner, with expression to help determine how it should be punctuated. Both children each rewrite the sentence using commas, capital letters, full stops, speech marks, apostrophes, questions marks and exclamation marks as necessary, to clarify meaning. The second child then reads the second sentence aloud and the process is repeated.

LA 🎴 **& SEN**

Individually, the children should read each sentence and then rewrite it, using accurate punctuation. **Support if required and/or scribe.**

Key Vocabulary

punctuation, capital letters, full stops, commas, apostrophes, question marks, exclamation marks, speech marks, sentence, complex sentences, connectives, adverbial phrases, adjectival phrases, possession, contraction

Plenary

Select children from each ability group to share their punctuated sentences on the board. You may need to scribe for some of them.

Check through the written sentences as a class, asking for suggestions as to any corrections that could be made.

Perfect Punctuation

✱ Rewrite these sentences in your book, adding the correct punctuation.

1. the door which was ajar slammed shut suddenly

2. bradley who was the driver stopped the car at the traffic lights which were red

3. eating five portions of fruit and vegetables stated mum is important to keep your body healthy

4. as soon as i get home whinged jay im getting out my x-box

5. in autumn when the leaves fall off the trees it is chilly and often windy

6. the baby who could not sleep was crying throughout the night

7. craig and gemma who were brother and sister fought like cat and dog

8. the wind which had begun to die down suddenly blew up again causing the leaves on the trees to tremble

✱ Now write some complex sentences of your own, making sure you punctuate them correctly.

I can use punctuation to clarify meaning in complex sentences. ☐

Snappy Slogans

Learning Objective

- To produce a poster advertising a product, using key features of the persuasion genre

Success Criteria

- I can produce a poster using the key features of persuasion genre.

CD-ROM Resources

- PowerPoint file
- Slide 4 in the PowerPoint file or an A3 copy of Resource Sheet 1
- Resource Sheet 2 for reference
- Copies of Resource Sheet 1

Other Resources

- Sheets of plain A4 paper
- Pencils
- Pens
- Coloured pencils (felt-tipped pens or gel pens are fine for writing, but not so good over large bands or areas of colour)

Introduction

Today we are going to make up a brand name for a product and a snappy slogan to sell it. Then we are going to make an advertising poster using the slogan and the key features of the persuasion genre.

What are the key features of advertisements?

Elicit and write on the board a list of the features: snappy slogans, exaggeration, intriguing questions, appealing adjectives, strong verbs and adverbs, wordplay, catchy rhymes, alliteration, humour, tempting descriptions of the product.

Can anyone give an example of each of these features?

For example:

- snappy slogan with alliteration: *The crisp with a crunch*
- exaggeration: *Crunchiest crisp on the planet*
- intriguing question with appealing adjective, strong verb, adverb: *Do you constantly crave a one-of-a-kind crisp?*
- Humour/word play/catchy rhyme: *Munch a crunchy crisp/Crunch a munchy crisp/Whatever you do, don't miss/A munch, crunch crisp like this!*
- tempting descriptions: *A delight in your mouth, tasty and healthy, made from the best quality potatoes*

Why do companies use them to sell their products?

They make you remember the product and want to try it.

Display the 'Track Trainers' advertisement (Resource Sheet 1) and discuss the key features. If showing a black and white copy, ask: *How might colour be used effectively?*

Point again to the key features of an advertisement listed on the board.

Why do we use different font styles and sizes, colour and so on?

Who is your audience?

Tell the children they are now going to annotate the key features of this 'Track Trainers' advertisement and then produce their own advertisement poster.

Activity

IN ABILITY GROUPS

AA

Working individually, the children should:

- annotate the key features using the advertisement;
- choose their own product to advertise;
- write the name in the centre of an A4 sheet and mind-map words and phrases, to use in the advertisement;
- write a snappy slogan for the product, using their mind-map;
- produce an advertisement poster using words and phrases from their mind-map and snappy slogan.

Extension: Write a letter to a shop trying to persuade them to stock their product.

MA

These children could do the same activity as above, working in pairs if they prefer. They should not be asked to do the extension activity.

LA & SEN

Working as a group with adult support, these children do the same activity but should:

- individually annotate the advertisement;
- be given suggestions for products if required and make a decision as a group;
- mind-map words and phrases, with an adult scribing;
- make up a slogan;
- individually produce a poster.

Key Vocabulary

advertisement, slogan, brand name, persuasion genre, key features, mind-map, exaggeration, intriguing questions, appealing adjective, strong verbs, adverbs, wordplay, catchy rhymes, alliteration, tempting

Plenary

Share and evaluate as many advertisements as possible. Ensure that a selection is made from each of the ability groups.

How could you improve it?

What key persuasion features have been used?

Would you buy it?

What would you change?

Snappy Slogans

intriguing question

alliteration

appealing adjective

exaggerated and tempting description

snappy slogan

appealing information

exaggeration

misleading - 90% of how many?

Want to run faster?

NEW
Track Trainers

These cool trainers will make you run like the wind!

- Special air cushion in soles for comfort
- Come in a range of funky colours
- Suitable for boys or girls

90% of the kids testing them said Track Trainers made them fly!!!!!

LIMITED EDITION – BUY NOW!!!

promoting urgency

Idioms Idiocy

Learning Objective

- To understand the difference between literal and figurative language, namely to show the literal meaning of an idiom

Success Criteria

- I can understand the difference between literal language and an idiom.

CD-ROM Resources

- PowerPoint file
- Slide 5 in the PowerPoint file or an enlarged copy of the Activity Sheet
- Copies of the Activity Sheet

Resources

- Highlighters
- Literacy books
- Pens
- Coloured pencils
- Glue

Introduction

Today we are going to going to look at figurative language and in particular at idioms.

What does 'figurative language' mean? Descriptive language used for interest and to help the audience understand how something looks or feels.

What does 'literal language' mean? It means exactly what it says.

What is an idiom?
Explain that an idiom is an everyday expression that cannot be literal (true). Idioms are used to make descriptions more interesting for the reader.

On the board, write 'She has eyes in the back of her head.' Draw a picture to illustrate it.

Does this mean that there are really eyes in the back of her head?

Explain that it is figurative language – an idiom.

What does it really mean? To seem to know everything that's happening around her.

What does 'make your eyes pop out' mean? Make you surprised.

NB. Some children with EAL or with specific learning difficulties will not understand the meaning of idioms and will need particular care during explanation.

Display the Activity Sheet and explain the activity.

Activity

AA
Individually, these children should highlight all the idioms in the 'Monday Morning' text, and then write another paragraph to continue the text, using at least three different idioms.

MA
Working in pairs, sharing ideas but recording individually, these children should highlight all of the idioms in the 'Monday Morning' text and then copy them, explaining each one beneath it.

LA & SEN
Working as a group supported by an adult, but recording individually, these children should highlight all of the idioms in the 'Monday Morning' text. A supporting adult should then discuss each one, helping the children to understand them.

Idioms used:	
shake a leg	bite my head off
bolt your food	eating out of my hand
packed in like sardines	keep that under your hat
a pain in the neck	back to square one
put the wind up	her bark is worse than her bite
a frog in the throat.	butter up
toe the line	big cheese
overstep the mark	get her knickers in a twist
	isn't my cup of tea

NB: If appropriate, the children can stick their highlighted Activity Sheet into their literacy book.

Key Vocabulary

figurative language, literal language, idiom, expression, descriptive, literal meaning, sentence, paragraph, simile, metaphor

Plenary

Ask the AA group to share their work with the class.

Which idioms did you highlight in the 'Monday Morning' story?

Which idioms did they use?

Were they used in context?

The MA and LA/SEN groups could share their suggestions for what each of the idioms might mean.

Explain to the children that, as with simile and metaphors, idioms can be used in their writing to make it interesting for the reader.

Idioms Idiocy

Monday Morning

"Shake a leg or you'll be late for school. Breakfast is on the table now. If you leave it any later, you will have to bolt your food!"

To be honest, I don't really care if I don't go to school at all. We will be packed in like sardines in the car and my younger brother (who's in Nursery) will be a pain in the neck, singing that silly nursery rhyme again. As usual, Mum will shout so loud she will put the wind up the baby and give herself a frog in the throat.

When we finally arrive at school, we will have to toe the line. If we overstep the mark, we will end up in trouble, and my teacher will bite my head off. Mind you, one big smile from me and she will soon be eating out of my hand. (Keep that last bit under your hat, though, or I will be back to square one!) Although it has to be said, her bark is worse than her bite.

There is a new child starting today. If I butter up the big cheese by offering to keep an eye on them, she may not get her knickers in a twist when I tell her that I haven't done my homework. Well, numeracy isn't my cup of tea.

Life Cycle of a Zog

Learning Objective

- To use knowledge of life cycles to produce one for an alien

Success Criteria

- I can use my knowledge of life cycles to create one for an alien animal.

CD-ROM Resources

- PowerPoint file
- Slide 4 in the PowerPoint file or an enlarged copy of Resource Sheet 1
- Slide 6 in the PowerPoint file or an enlarged copy of Resource Sheet 2
- Slide 7 in the PowerPoint file or an enlarged copy of Resource Sheet 3
- Copies of Resource Sheets 1, 2 and 3

Other Resources

- A3 plain paper for designs
- Lined paper for data files
- Pencils
- Rubbers
- Coloured pencils
- Pens for labelling and writing

Introduction

Today we are going to revise the human life cycle and then use this knowledge to produce a life cycle for an alien called a Zog from the planet Sram. (Mars backwards)

Why is it called a life cycle?
Because it represents the stages of life as a circle from embryo to adult to embryo.

What are the stages of a human life cycle?
Embryo in womb, Baby, Child, Adolescent, Adult.

Show the picture of the Life Cycle of a Human (Resource Sheet 1).

Who can draw a line to match one of the labels to the correct picture of the stage?

Repeat until all pictures are correctly labelled.

Explain to the children that they are going to use their knowledge of the human life cycle to produce one for an alien. Remind them that an alien life cycle won't necessarily be like a human one.

Show the picture of the adult Zog (Resource Sheet 2) and explain that the children will be creating the other three stages of its life cycle, and a data file to accompany it.

Show the partially-completed Zog data file (Resource Sheet 3), emphasising that this is just an example, and the children must think of their own ideas and names.

What do you think 'pringoes' and 'poogs' are?
Perhaps units of measure for life span – e.g. weeks and months, or months and years.

What else besides life span do we need to consider when we are making up the Zog Life Cycle?
Brainstorm ideas and list them on the board:

- what it looks like at full maturity
- habitat
- diet
- egg or live birth
- how it could develop
- how many stages (in this case, 4)
- names for each stage

Leave on display.
Explain the activity.

Activity

AA
Individually, the children should design the other three stages of the life cycle of a Zog, draw and label each each stage of the life cycle, and produce a data file for it.

MA
Working in pairs but recording individually, these children should design the other three stages of the life cycle of a Zog, then draw and label each stage of the life cycle.
Extension: Create a data file.

LA & SEN
In pairs, these children should design the other three stages of the life cycle of a Zog and draw and label each stage. **With support as necessary.**

Key Vocabulary

life cycle, human, embryo, womb, baby, child, adolescent, adult, life, death, maturity, reproduction, stages, habitat, diet, life span, egg, live birth, develop

Plenary

Share a selection of work from each ability group.

Display the Success Criteria on the board.

Have they addressed each issue?

Does the cycle look plausible?

How could they have improved on their design?

If there is time, as a class design a life cycle for a completely new species of insect.

Life Cycle of a Zog

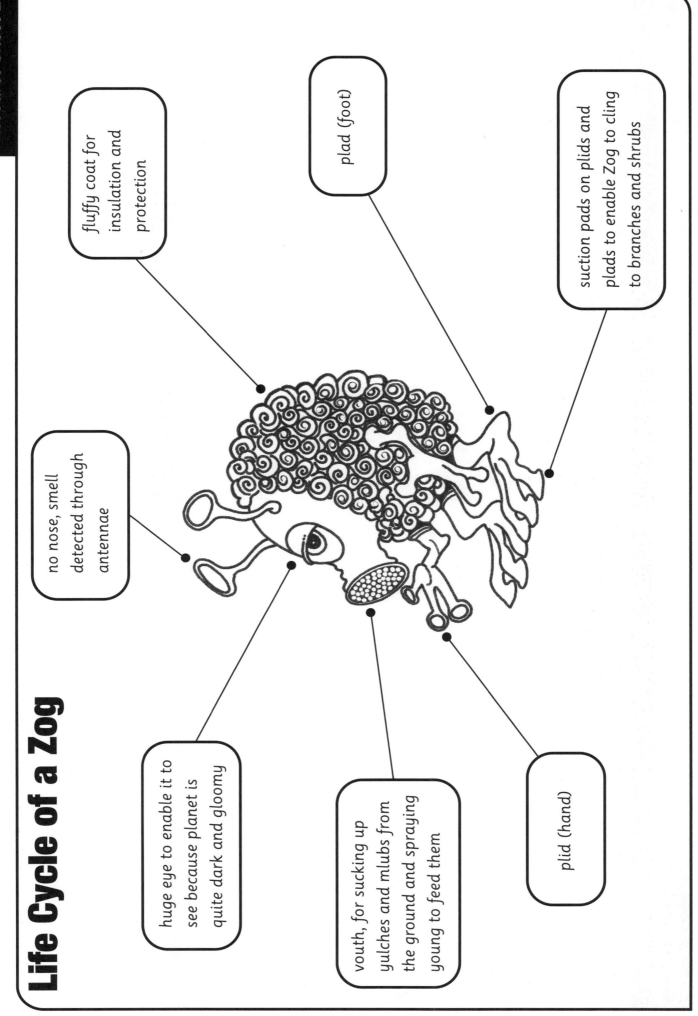

fluffy coat for insulation and protection

plad (foot)

suction pads on plids and plads to enable Zog to cling to branches and shrubs

no nose, smell detected through antennae

huge eye to enable it to see because planet is quite dark and gloomy

vouth, for sucking up yulches and mlubs from the ground and spraying young to feed them

plid (hand)

Simply Science

Simply Solar

Learning Objective	Introduction	Activity	Plenary
• To develop knowledge and understanding through using a range of sources of information and data	*Today we are going to read about asteroids, meteoroids and comets, identifying the key features of information texts, and then take part in a quiz about what we have read.* Begin by asking the children what they already know about the solar system. Continue with a shared reading of the text 'Asteroids, Meteoroids and Comets' (Resource Sheet 1). Discuss any vocabulary that is new to the children. *What are the key features of an information text?* Write them on the board, adding any below that are not included. Key Features of Information Texts: • A general introduction • Subheadings • Bullet points or numbering of points • Present tense • Time and causal connectives (because, to, this causes) • Non-chronological (not listed in order of time of events) • Impersonal language • Specific information/data • Clear points • Technical vocabulary • Last sentence of each topic contains a conclusion • Labelled diagrams and/or captioned pictures • Question Explain to the children that not all texts will necessarily contain every feature in the list. Explain the activity.	The children should work in mixed-ability pairs for five minutes to reread the text and highlight all the key features. Remind them that they are going to have a quiz on what they have read, so they need to concentrate on the actual content too. **Playing the quiz** Split the children into a number of mixed-ability teams. The teams will compete against each other in a quiz, answering questions on the text they have just read. First, the teams should elect a scribe to write down the answers. Then the teams should be given one or two minutes to think of a team name and write it at the top of their answer sheet. The teacher should read out the questions from Resource Sheet 2, allowing sufficient time for the teams to find the information and write the answer. The final question is optional, or can be used as an extension activity.	The teacher should read out each question and give the correct answer. The teams can mark their own answers or swap and mark another team's answers. Tally the scores to find the winning team. Optional question 23: *How many new words did you find?* If time, work through them and check the spelling. Ask a few children to share what was the most interesting fact they learned.

Success Criteria

• I can use an information text to learn about asteroids, meteoroids and comets and answer questions about them.

CD-ROM Resources

• PowerPoint file
• Slide 3 in the PowerPoint file or an enlarged copy of Resource Sheet 1
• Copies of Resource Sheet 1
• Master copy of the quiz – with answers (Resource Sheet 2)

Other Resources

• Highlighters
• Paper and pens/pencils

Key Vocabulary

asteroids, meteoroids, comets, minor planets, meteors, meteorite, orbit/ing, Sun, Earth, Earth's atmosphere, nucleus, gas, dust, ice, impact craters

Simply Solar

Asteroids, Meteoroids and Comets

Asteroids are pieces of rock and iron that orbit the big star we call the Sun. Meteoroids are smaller bits of material that fly through space. Comets orbit the Sun, and are made of ice, dust and rock.

Asteroids

Asteroids are sometimes known as 'minor planets' although they can range in size from a few metres across to almost 1000km (621 miles) wide. Many asteroids are found orbiting in an asteroid belt between Mars and Jupiter. Over 9000 asteroids have been located and named.

Meteoroids

Meteoroids travel at great speed. When they enter Earth's atmosphere, they burn up due to friction with the air. These streaks of light are called meteors, or shooting stars. If meteors don't burn up completely, due to their large size, they hit Earth's surface. These are called meteorites. The Barrington Crater in Arizona, USA, was formed when a 30-50 metre iron meteorite hit Earth about 50 000 years ago. It is one of about 120 impact craters on Earth.

Comets

There are billions of comets orbiting the Sun. A comet doesn't have a tail for most of its orbit. As a comet moves closer to the Sun, it begins to warm up. Gas and dust from the nucleus, or solid icy centre of the comet, begin to form a cloud or a 'coma' around the nucleus. The Sun and its solar wind blow the coma into two tails, one of gas and one of dust. As the comet moves away from the Sun, the tails shrink.

A comet's tail can be thousands of kilometers long

DID YOU KNOW?
Halley's comet last visited Earth in 1986.

Halley's comet is the best known periodic comet with the first recorded sighting being in China in 240BC. It returns to Earth every 75-76 years. Its next visit to the inner solar system will be the summer of 2061.

A crater created from the impact of an asteroid

Mark Making – Van Gogh

Learning Objectives

- To learn how to use visual and tactile elements such as pattern and lines to achieve a certain effect
- To recreate a section of a picture utilising mark-making skills

Success Criteria

- I can recreate a section of picture using mark-making skills.

CD-ROM Resources

- PowerPoint file
- Slide 3 in the PowerPoint file or an enlarged copy of the Resource Sheet
- Copies of the Resource Sheet

Other Resources

- Scrap paper to experiment with marks
- A5 paper for picture
- A6 paper cut up for viewfinders
- Clear sticky tape to secure viewfinder
- HB pencils
- Scissors

Introduction

Today we are going to recreate a section of a picture using mark-making skills.

Who can tell me what mark making is?
Drawing or painting a picture using a series of marks.

Display the Resource Sheet. Study the Van Gogh line drawing closely.

Tell the children a little about Van Gogh.

- 19th-century Dutch painter, born in 1853 and died in 1890 at the early age of 37
- During a period of mental ill health, he cut off part of his left ear
- He made around 900 paintings in only 10 years, but sold only one during his lifetime
- He became famous after his death for his paintings that used broad, broken brush strokes

Can you tell me what is different about this sketch from other sketches that you have seen?

Discuss the fact that Van Gogh has used different techniques of mark making to draw his picture. Explain that he also used this technique of mark making in his paintings.

An HB pencil, the type you use for writing, has a hard lead. How many different stokes/techniques do you think you can get from it?

Demonstrate how to use the very tip for a dark, hard line. Use gently for a softer, less dark line. Use the pencil flat to the paper so that the line produced gives a soft, thick line. Now repeat but with pressure to get a thick, dark line that you can smudge with your finger.

Let the children practise these techniques on some scrap paper, going round the whole class helping where required.

NB: This lesson can be extended by enlarging the picture, using bolder/bigger marks, strips of paper or using paint.

Activity

ALL ABILITIES

Give each child an A6 piece of paper and scissors. Demonstrate making a viewfinder by folding in half and cutting a 1cm square from the middle fold. The children then select a portion of the Van Gogh picture that they want to reproduce, open the viewfinder and place it over the picture until that part shows in the middle of the viewfinder. They then stick it in place. When they have finished that, they should reproduce that portion of the sketch, enlarging it to fill an entire A5 sheet.

The teacher should circulate, supporting the children and showing examples of good work as it is done.

The children should evaluate their own work, and then swap with a partner to evaluate each other's.

Have I included the techniques I learned?

Is it an accurate representation of what I can see?

Have I drawn it with care?

How can I improve it?

Extension: Make another small picture of your own using similar marks.

Key Vocabulary

line, mark making, mark-making skills, strokes, techniques, pattern

Plenary

Share a selection of the work the children have done.

Ask the class to evaluate each sketch using the questions in the Activity column, which could be written on the board.

Positive feedback should be given first, and then constructive criticism.

Did they enjoy this exercise? Would they like to try it with a different painting?

Mark Making – Van Gogh

Van Gogh's 'Entrance Gate to a Farm with Haystacks' (Reproduced by permission of Rijksmuseum.)

Design a Clock

Learning Objectives

- To use a variety of methods and approaches to communicate observations and design ideas
- To design a clock

Success Criteria

- I can design a clock.

CD-ROM Resources

- PowerPoint file
- Slide 4 in the PowerPoint file or an enlarged copy of Resource Sheet 1
- Slide 5 in the PowerPoint file or an enlarged copy of Resource Sheet 2
- Slide 6 in the PowerPoint file or an enlarged copy of Resource Sheet 3

Other Resources

- A3 paper for design
- A4 paper for the drawing of the end product
- Pencils, coloured pencils or felt-tipped pens

Introduction

Today we are going to design a clock.

What features does a clock need?

For example: analogue or digital clockface; hour and minute hands; sometimes a second hand; either numbers or another device to denote the hours; sometimes divisions for minutes; a way of working – mechanical (wind up, pendulum), electronic (mains electricity, battery)

Look at the selection of different clocks (Resource Sheet 1).

What features do these clocks have?

Discuss the features of each:
What shape is it?
Can you see the hands clearly?
How easy is it to tell the time on them? Why?
Do they all have the hours marked on them?
What material do you think it is made from?

Explain to the children that they are going to design their own clock. It may be any type they like, but must be planned in detail and labelled. Display and discuss the example of a labelled design (Resource Sheet 2).

Display the list of questions below (Resource Sheet 3) to help them. Read it through with them.

- What shape will your clock be?
- Will it be analogue or digital?
- Is your clock going to have all the numbers, a few or none?
- What materials will it be made from?
- What components will be needed?
- What size and colour will the components be?
- How will they be attached?
- What room will it be intended for?
- Will it be wall-mounted or stand-alone?
- What special features are required; for example, chimes, battery or pendulum?

Can you think of any other questions to ask during the design process?

Add any suggestions to the list.

Activity

ALL ABILITY GROUPS

The children should first experiment with their own different shapes and designs using sketches and labelling before they produce their final design. Each sketch should then be evaluated by asking the questions displayed.

The children should design with care and attention to detail. The designs must be labelled and details of materials that would be used are to be included.

Once completed, the children can evaluate their own work.

Does it fulfil all the requirements?
Have I answered all the questions on the list displayed?
How can I improve it?

Extension ideas

The children could produce a list of the resources required. They could estimate the cost to produce the clock and a retail price in order to make a profit.

Key Vocabulary

design process, features, material, pendulum, contemporary, plate, components, requirements

Plenary

Select different children to share their clock designs with the class.

Ask the class to evaluate it.

Does it fulfil all the requirements?

How can I improve it?

(See the questions on the displayed list.)

The class should be able to give one positive comment and one constructive criticism.

How would the list of questions change if they were going to design a watch or a grandfather clock?

Design a Clock

Clock dial

- shaped like book
- size: 30cm wide x 22cm deep
- aluminium dial
- painted primary green with acrylic paint
- page markings in black

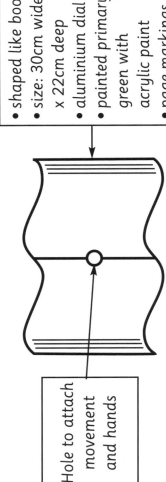

Hole to attach movement and hands

Hands

Hour hand
- shaped like pencil
- yellow
- rigid plastic
- black markings
- 1.5cm wide x 5cm long

brown

hole to attach to dial

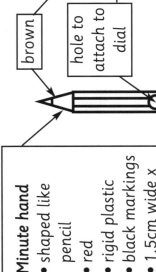

Minute hand
- shaped like pencil
- red
- rigid plastic
- black markings
- 1.5cm wide x 8cm long

Numbers and Markers

- white rigid plastic for main hour numbers
- height: 4cm

1 2 3 6 9

- white rigid plastic markers for remaining hours
- height: 3cm

Movement

hook to mount on wall

dial to alter time

battery holder

- black, rigid plastic, enclosed case containing movement
- size: 9cm x 6cm x 3.5cm

The Trial of Isabella Thomas

Learning Objectives	Introduction	Activity	Plenary
• To understand about the experiences of children's lives in Victorian times • To role-play a Victorian trial	**Today we are going to investigate what happened to child offenders in Victorian times.** **What does the word offence mean?** Crime **Offender?** Someone who commits a crime.	**Teacher's Notes** • Allocate parts for the children to play. The roles of the jurors and characters with the largest speaking parts should be given to the more able at speaking and listening. LA and SEN children may need coaching or be given roles as guards, who say nothing. • Depending on the size of the class, the children can double up on parts, or more parts can be added.	Discuss the outcome of the trial. Does everyone think that it was a fair trial and that the outcome was the right one? **What do you think it was like for poor children in Victorian times?** **What kind of life do you think Isabella might have had if she were not poor?** **What are the differences between how children were treated in Victorian times and today?**

Success Criteria

• I can understand about the experiences of children's lives in Victorian times.

Can you tell me some acts that are illegal? List them on the board. Include stealing, vandalism and graffiti.

What are the consequences of committing an offence today? Ask the children to discuss this in pairs and then share ideas as a whole class. (Possible answers: a caution, court and sentence, ASBO, probation.)

What does judicial system mean? The system that deals with enforcing the law.

• Write the names of the children playing each part on the Cast List sheet (Resource Sheet 3).
• Give the children their appropriate role-play briefs (Resource Sheets 4 and 5) and allow them five minutes or so to read them and get into character.
• Announce the beginning of the trial by saying, for example, "The trial of Isabella Thomas is now in session. Judge [name of child] presiding." Your role is to ensure that a good pace for the role-play is maintained (and, if there are too few children in the class, to act as Clerk of the Court, calling the witnesses to take the stand).

CD-ROM Resources

• PowerPoint file
• Slide 5 in the PowerPoint file or an enlarged copy of Resource Sheet 1
• Slide 6 in the PowerPoint file or an enlarged copy of Resource Sheet 2
• Copy of the cast list (Resource Sheet 3)
• 2 copies of the Role-play Briefs – one cut up into character slips, one to use for stage prompting (Resource Sheets 4 and 5)

How would vandalism be dealt with today?

How do you think it would have been dealt with in Victorian times?

Repeat this for anti-social behaviour.

What was the judicial system like in Victorian times? Display the Information Sheet (Resource Sheet 1). Discuss or explain, reminding the children that life was really harsh for poor children then. Unlike today, they had no rights.

Display The Bedford County Gaol Register (Resource Sheet 2). Look at the prison record of Isabella Thomas. (The name and record are fictitious, but details have been taken from a number of real records.)

Why do you think she might have stolen bread and oranges?

Explain that the class is now going to act out Isabella's trial.

• Jurors' instructions are role-play guidance. They can ad-lib during the deliberations, in character.
• Other characters have their speech on their briefing slips. They should actually say whatever is on the slip.
• For less mature classes, if appropriate, the teacher can play the role of the judge.
• At the end, allow five minutes for the jury to deliberate (discuss in role) in front of the class. This will enable the rest of the class to be aware of the process.
• The class can then vote with the judge on Isabella's sentence, if she is found guilty.

Key Vocabulary

flogging, whipping, hard labour, transportation, reformatory school (correction), gruel, Victorian, gaol, dock, costermonger (sold fruit, vegetables and fish from a cart), cobbler, butler, needlewoman, workhouse, milk maid, stable boy, mill owner, music hall, boro' sessions

The Trial of Isabella Thomas

Bedford County Gaol Register

Isabella Thomas

Name .... Isabella Thomas

Description

Age .... 11 years
Height .... 4ft 2 inches
Hair .... Brown
Eyes .... Hazel
Visage .... Sallow
Weight .... –
Trade .... None
Place of birth .... Hatfield, Herts
Last residence .... Hatfield
Married or single ...... Single
Religion .... Church of England
Read and write .... No

Marks and Birth marks:

Scar on forehead

Mole on left cheek

Offence:

Stealing a loaf of bread and two oranges

When tried:

Boro' Sessions 21st November 1874

Water, Water Everywhere

Learning Objectives

- To use a secondary source of information (poem) to understand the process of the water cycle
- To interpret and explain the process through drawing

Success Criteria

- I understand the process of the water cycle and the effect of water on the landscape.

CD-ROM Resources

- PowerPoint file
- Slide 5 in the PowerPoint file or an enlarged copy of the Resource Sheet ('Water cycle' poem)
- Copies of the differentiated Activity Sheets for 🎲 and 🎲

Other Resources

- Highlighter pens
- Drawing paper for 🎲 group
- Pens, pencils, crayons, coloured pencils

Introduction

Today we are going to read a poem and use the information in it as a starting point for discussing and showing our understanding of the water cycle.

What do you already know about the water cycle?

Spend a few minutes determining the children's prior knowledge of the subject. Write any relevant vocabulary on the board – for example, vapour, evaporate, condense, cloud, river, rainfall, and so on.

Tell the children you are going to read them a poem about the water cycle. Read the poem (Resource Sheet) through expressively, but do not, at this point, show them the poem. Now, read it again, asking the children to listen out for subject-specific vocabulary.

Do you think this is a good description of the water cycle? Why or why not?

Now display the poem.

What is unusual about the poem?

It is a shape (or concrete) poem.

Why do you think the poet chose this format?

Because it reflects the circular process of the water cycle.

Discuss with the children how the poem is not only a great example of rhyming, shape poetry with figurative language, but it also conveys factual information about a physical, environmental process.

Where does water come from?
Where does water go?
How are rivers formed?

Leave the poem on display for the children to refer to during the activity.

Explain the activity.

Activity

AA 🎲

These children should work individually to communicate the factual information in the poem as a labelled pictorial diagram of the water cycle. They should use appropriate vocabulary. Encourage them to use the poem as reference.

Extension: On the back of their diagram, the children could answer the question: What are the effects of too much water (flooding) or too little water (drought)?

MA 🎲

These children should be given Activity Sheet 🎲 and asked to label the drawing, explaining briefly the stages of the water cycle and using appropriate vocabulary. Encourage them to use the poem as reference. They should work individually.

Extension: On the back of their diagram, the children could answer the question: Where does the water you use every day come from?

LA 🎲 and SEN 🎲

These children should be given Activity Sheet 🎲 and asked to work in pairs to match the numbered statements at the bottom of the sheet to the boxes within the diagram. They should write the statement number in the appropriate box.

With support as appropriate.

Extension: On the back of the sheet, the children could draw and label pictures of how they use water (e.g. drinking, bathing, watering the garden, swimming).

Key Vocabulary

water cycle, vapour, evaporate, rain, hail, snow, condense, cloud, soil, lake, river, sea, ocean, tributary

Plenary

Share the children's work, selecting children from each ability group to present their diagrams.

Did they find the poem helpful in drawing and labelling their diagram? Why or why not?

Display the poem again. As a class, select and highlight the words or phrases that they were able to use in their diagrams.

Discuss the Extension questions:

What are the effects of too much water (flooding) or too little water (drought)?

Where does the water you use every day come from?

Give examples of how you use water in your daily life.

Water, Water Everywhere

Clouds in the sky
Look like paper
But made up of vapour,
Drift over the hills
Where the air chills.
Vapour condenses,
Rainfall commences
(Or dew on the grass
Like breath on a glass)
This trickles to give us
Streamlets and rivers
Till by degrees

* Start

Noel Petty

* Riding on high,
All over again.
Ready to rain
Into the skies
Then the mists rise
By the sun's rays.
Of watery haze
Allows the creation
And evaporation
Gradually heats it
There the sun greets it
It reaches the seas.

Vivaldi

Learning Objectives	Introduction	Activity	Plenary
• To listen to and talk about the atmosphere and mood created by a piece of music • To compare and contrast two concertos by Vivaldi	*Today we are going to compare two concertos composed by Vivaldi.* Remind/explain some musical terms: **tempo** – variations in speed **timbre** – quality of the sound; for example: jerky, joyful, stirring, bracing, soothing **dynamics** – variation in volume, usually loud or quiet **structure** – how sounds are organised – beginning, middle and end, repetition **ostinato/ostinati** (plural) – short rhythmic pattern/s repeated over and over **concerto** – composition for solo (single) instrument and orchestra	**MIXED ABILITY GROUPS** Working independently or in pairs. Tell the children they will now concentrate on the elements featured on the Activity Sheet: tempo, timbre, dynamics, structure. Let them listen to the music again for each element, completing each remaining section of the sheet when directed by the teacher, (after discussion, unless the answer is personal preference). When they have completed the sheet for 'Spring Allegro', they should then listen to 'Winter Largo' and repeat the above activity.	***What happens in Spring?*** Mind-map ideas on the board; for example, new growth, starting to play outside. ***Does Vivaldi's music reflect this season?*** ***What happens in Winter?*** Mind-map on the board again; for example, hot dinners to keep out the cold, wanting to play inside to keep warm, dark nights. Discuss as a whole class: ***Does Vivaldi's music reflect this season?*** ***Did you enjoy the concertos? Why? Which did you prefer and why?***

Success Criteria

• I can compare and contrast two concertos by Vivaldi.

Listen as a whole class to 'Spring Allegro'. Remind them of the definition of the musical terms again.

Complete the first part of the activity together as a whole class in order to demonstrate how the other parts should be completed. Listen to the music again.

What is the tempo of this piece? Fast or slow?

Discuss their feelings as a whole class.

Does it make you feel sleepy or excited?

Write their ideas on the board.

LA & SEN

The teacher should support if appropriate.

CD-ROM Resources

• PowerPoint file
• Audio tracks from Vivaldi's *Four Seasons*: 'Spring Allegro (1st)' and 'Winter Largo'
• Class copies of Comparison Sheet (Activity Sheet)
• Copy of Answers Sheet

Key Vocabulary

concerto, concertos, composed, composer, tempo, timbre, dynamics, structure, ostinato, ostinati, piece, comparison, compare, reflect

Comparing Vivaldi's Spring and Winter Concertos

	Spring	Winter
tempo		
timbre		
dynamics		
structure		
What happens in this season?		
Does Vivaldi's music reflect the season?		
Did you enjoy this concerto and why?		
Which do you prefer? Why?		

tempo – variations in speed   **timbre** – quality of the sound e.g. jerky, joyful, stirring, bracing, soothing   **dynamics** – variation in volume, usually loud or quiet
structure – how sounds organised: beg, middle and end, repetition   **ostinato/ostinati** (plural) – short rhythmic pattern/s repeated over and over
concerto – composition for solo (single) instrument and orchestra

Carnival of the Animals

Learning Objective

- To explore and compare the musical elements in two movements of Saint-Saens' *Carnival of the Animals*

Success Criteria

- I can explore and compare the musical elements in two pieces of music.

CD-ROM Resources

- Audio tracks of 'Elephants' and 'Aquarium' from *Carnival of the Animals* by Camille Saint-Saens
- PowerPoint file
- Slide 5 in the PowerPoint file or an enlarged copy of Resource Sheet 1
- Copy of Resource Sheet 2
- Copies of the Activity Sheet

Other Resources

- Coloured pencils
- Rulers

Introduction

Today we are going to compare the musical elements in two pieces of music.

Explain that the two pieces of music come from *Carnival of the Animals* by the French composer Camille Saint-Saens, and that each of these two pieces describes different animals.

Introduce/revise some music terminology:
Who can tell me what the word 'dynamics' means?
Variation in volume – e.g. loud, soft

Repeat with:

rhythm – beat of the sound

tempo – variations in speed, e.g. fast, slow

timbre – quality or mood of the sound, e.g. jerky, joyful, stirring, bracing, soothing

pitch – range of sounds, low to high

structure – how sounds are organised, e.g. beginning, middle and end, repetition

ostinato – short, rhythmic pattern that repeats

Display the Musical Elements (Resource Sheet 1) for the children to refer to.

Play the 'Elephants' track.
Did you like it?

What instruments did you hear? (Piano and double bass)
What animal do you think this piece of music describes? (Elephant)

Now play the track again and ask the children to listen carefully and think about the dynamics, rhythm, tempo, timbre, pitch and structure. (You may wish to select just a few of the elements for the children to focus on.)

Discuss the elements, writing the children's responses on the board, if appropriate. If necessary, use the information on the Teacher Information – Elements sheet (Resource Sheet 2) to prompt the children's discussion. If there is time, play the piece again during the course of the discussion to help children focus on the elements.

Explain the activity.

Activity

IN MIXED ABILITY GROUPS

Working individually, or in pairs or groups (depending on your preference or the appropriateness for the class), the children should first fill in the top part of the Activity Sheet as a record of the discussion about 'Elephants' in the Introduction. Allow about 10 minutes for this.

Explain that they are now going to listen to another piece of music from *Carnival of the Animals* called 'Aquarium'. (Ensure they understand what 'aquarium' means.) They should listen carefully and, using the bottom part of the Activity Sheet, describe the elements in the same way they did for 'Elephants'.

If possible, play the track several times to help focus the children's attention and promote thinking time.

LA & SEN

Support if appropriate, particularly with scribing.

Key Vocabulary

musical elements, dynamics, rhythm, tempo, pitch, timbre, structure, instruments

Plenary

Ask selected children to share their answers to questions 6–12 on the Activity Sheet.

In discussing responses to questions 11 and 12, emphasise the fact that there are no right or wrong answers to those. Music evokes different responses in different people and they are all equally valid.

Explain to the children that there are actually 14 different pieces of music that make up *Carnival of the Animals*. Suggest to them that they might like to find and listen to the other pieces.

Carnival of the Animals

Elephants

1. What instruments did you hear in this piece? _____

_____

2. What is the underlying rhythm? _____

_____

3. How does the tempo reflect the different characteristics of elephants?

_____

4. What words can you think of to describe the timbre (mood) of this piece?

_____

5. Describe briefly the structure of 'Elephants'. _____

_____

Aquarium

6. The track begins with an (element term) _____that is _____
   repeated throughout the piece.

7. Describe it. _____

_____

8. Describe the tempo of this track. _____

_____

9. What words can you think of to describe the timbre of the track? _____

_____

10. What instruments play the bubbles and water? _____

_____

11. Which track do you prefer, 'Elephants' or 'Aquarium'? _____

_____

12. Give your reasons. (Continue on the back of this sheet if necessary.)

_____

I can explore and compare musical elements in two pieces of music. ☐

Let's Make Money

Learning Objective	Introduction	Activity	Plenary
• To look after your money and realise that future wants and needs may be met by saving	*Today we are going to learn how to make more money by not spending it.*	**CHILDREN TO WORK IN PAIRS**	*How much do you think you could regularly save from your pocket money?*
Success Criteria	*What is the difference between wants and needs?* Needs: food, shelter, water, heat, light for survival. Wants: new designer sweatshirt or trainers, mobile phone and so on	Display the 'My Money Tracker' sheet (Resource Sheet) and talk the children through how the different rows and columns work. Tell them that they will be designing their own tracker sheet, but first they are going to use the My Financial Plan sheet (Activity Sheet) to answer the following questions:	*What ideas did you think of to earn some more money?*
• I can design a balance sheet to help me keep track of my money.	*What do you spend your pocket money on?* *What happens when you want to buy something that is too expensive?* *What sort of things would you like to buy but cannot afford?*	What is it I want to buy? How much will it cost? How can I make/save the money to buy it?	*What is it you want to save for?* *How long do you think it would take you?*
CD-ROM Resources	*How could you earn a bit more money for things like bowling, swimming, the cinema, presents, holidays and other large expenses?*	Leave the money tracker sheet on display as a template for them to design their own so that they can keep track of their income, expenditure and balance.	
• PowerPoint file • Slide 5 in the PowerPoint file or an A3 copy of the Resource Sheet • Copies of the Activity Sheet, cut into 2	By doing odd jobs for family and friends, such as washing cars, and saving money received as gifts for birthdays and special occasions. Emphasise to the children that any job that involves people outside the family must have parental permission and should never be done alone.	**LA & SEN** Provide peer support or teacher support, whichever is appropriate.	
	Explain that, as adults, they will have lots of large expenses to pay for. Often adults will borrow money on which they have to pay a lot of interest, which is an extra amount of money on top of what they have borrowed, and that is why people often get into debt, and worry about it.		
Other Resources	Suggest that saving a little each week would mean that they would be able to afford those 'wants' and is very good practice for when they are older. Explain that they could put their savings in a piggy bank, but if they save with a bank or building society by opening a children's account, they will actually get interest on their savings, which means money added for nothing. While many offer incentives such as free gifts or vouchers for opening an account, it is best to go for the one that pays the most interest. You can earn a higher rate of interest if you open an account that doesn't allow withdrawals (taking money out) without notice (warning).	**Key Vocabulary**	
• Lined paper • Pens • Pencils • Rulers	Go through the Key Vocabulary list of words with the children and then explain the activity.	**money, loans, instalments, savings, accounts, banks, building societies, deposits, withdrawals, expenses, income, credit, debit, interest, wants, needs, incentives, interest rates**	

Let's Make Money

My Money Tracker

Date	Description	Credit		Debit		Balance	
5 September	Pocket money	5	00			5	00
5 September	Savings account			2	00	3	00
12 September	Birthday money from Aunty Sharon	10	00			13	00
14 September	Cinema			5	00	8	00
18 September	Savings account			5	00	3	00
24 September	Washed Dad's car	6	00			9	00
28 September	Ice cream and drink			3	25	5	75

Carnival of the Animals

Learning Objective

- To explore and explain their own ideas and feelings about music using movement and dance

Success Criteria

- I can explore the elements of 'Elephants' and 'Aquarium' from *The Carnival of the Animals* through movement and dance.

CD-ROM Resources

- Audio tracks of 'Elephants' and 'Aquarium' from *Carnival of the Animals* by Camille Saint-Saens

NB: There is no PowerPoint file for this lesson as it is assumed the lesson will take place in the hall.

Other Resources

- CD player
- Whistle to attract attention

Introduction

Today we are going to choreograph and perform some phrases using music that depicts different animal characters from some music called Carnival of the Animals.

What does 'to choreograph' mean? To compose a sequence of dance steps, in this case, to music.

What do 'phrases' mean? Short sequences of movement.

Tell the children that dance is a form of drama, but using movement and facial expressions instead of words.

Close your eyes and imagine you are seeing a herd of elephants. What are the features of an elephant? Heavy body, large cumbersome legs and feet, long flexible trunk, large ears that flap to keep it cool, short tail.

How does it move? Heavily, lumbering, stately, grandly, proudly, swinging its trunk.

Play the music for the elephants from *Carnival of the Animals*.

Think about how elephants might move if they were to dance a slow dance (waltz). Is this music good for describing that? Think about how you might compose a dance for this.

Allow a minute for the children to think.

What is an aquarium? What different animals might you see in one? Different types of fish in a range of colours and sizes. *What else will you see?* Water and plants.

Now, close your eyes and imagine you can see an aquarium. How are the fish moving? Some slowly and gracefully, gliding and swaying, with short bursts of speed; others in shoals, darting about, some peeping out from their hiding places. *What about the water and plants?* Bubbling, flowing and trickling; swaying.

Play the music for the aquarium.

Is this music good for describing an aquarium? Did you hear music that described how fish move? How the water and plants move? Think about how you might compose a dance for this piece of music.

Activity

IN MIXED ABILITY GROUPS

Warm up by stretching out your bodies as if you were an elephant stretching its trunk to reach the top of a tree, then shrinking down small, and then stretching out again.

Play the elephants music. The children should:

- In pairs, explore the characteristics and actions of an elephant in time to the music, being aware of others. They should vary and develop their actions (not forgetting the elephant's trunk) using the space around them sensibly.
- In groups, combine ideas within their group to produce a short phrase to the music. They should vary body shape, height, group size and directions within their phrase, while responding and keeping in time with the music when performing.

Repeat this with the music for the aquarium. Ask the children to think about which type of fish they are, darting and hiding or swimming gracefully. Or will they choose to be plants swaying in the water, or the water bubbling upwards and trickling down again?

Cool down by standing on the spot and swaying as if you were being pulled by the water in different directions.

NB: Safety issues

- Remove all jewellery and cover any earrings that cannot be removed.
- Wear shoes while walking to and from the hall.
- Remind children to be mindful of other people's space when dancing.

Key Vocabulary

choreograph, perform, phrases, sequences, movement, drama, facial expressions, characteristics

Plenary

How effective were your movements when you were elephants dancing?

You could ask one pair to demonstrate what they did.

How could you change the movements to improve your choreography?

How effective were your movements as fish in an aquarium? Did anyone prefer to portray the movement of the water and plants? How did you do that?

Again, ask one child or pair to demonstrate what they did.

Which music and movement did you prefer, elephants or aquarium?

Saint-Saens, who wrote the music, wrote pieces for 14 different creatures including a lion and a swan. Can you imagine how these creatures might move?

Success Criteria

I can explore the elements of 'The Elephants' and 'Aquarium' through movement and dance.

✔ I can think about the characteristics and movements of elephants and fish, and explore these through dance, in response to the changes in the music

✔ I can remember to use my facial expressions, head and hands as well as my limbs to portray them.

✔ I can work with my group to produce and perform a short dance phrase to represent them.

Supply Teacher Feedback Form

Class:

Supply Teacher's Name:

Date:

Class behaviour: (please circle)

Excellent	**Good**	**Satisfactory**	**Unsatisfactory/Poor**

Incidents:

Maths:

☺ Excelled:

☹ Struggled:

Literacy:

☺ Excelled:

☹ Struggled:

Other subjects:

☺ Excelled:

☹ Struggled:

Other subjects:

☺ Excelled:

☹ Struggled:

Additional information/General comments:

Signed:

Supply Teacher Feedback Form – Sample

Class: 5C-Q
Date: 21/11/2009

Supply Teacher's Name: Candy Adler

Class behaviour: (please circle)

(Excellent)　　　　　**Good**　　　　　**Satisfactory**　　　　　**Unsatisfactory/Poor**

Incidents: Steven hit Zac. Spoke to him and made him apologise.
Amy refused to do independent work today.

Maths: To recall multiplication facts by completing puzzle (10 x 10)

☺ Excelled: Louis, Jade, Samir, Kieran, Amber, Safia

☹ Struggled: Ethan, Daisy, Tyler, Amy

Literacy: To punctuate sentences accurately including speech marks

☺ Excelled: Demi, Kyle, Jessica, Shannon, Kieran, Bailey

☹ Struggled: Ethan, Daisy, Tyler, Amy

Other subjects: PE/Dance – To explore ideas and feelings about music using movement and dance

☺ Excelled: Gemma, Ewan, Scott

☹ Struggled: Jamie, Toni, Samira

Other subjects: Geography – To use four-figure grid references on a map

☺ Excelled: Natalia, Alessandro, Sara

☹ Struggled: Ashleigh, Kyle, Amy

Additional information/General comments:

I had a lovely day with your class!

Signed:

Maths

Tables Teaser Puzzles

[1]1	2	[2]1	▓	[3]9	6	▓	[4]1	0	[5]8
6	▓	[6]4	0	▓	[7]7	2	▓		1
▓	[8]2	4	▓		[9]7	0	▓	▓	
[10]8	4	▓	[11]2	[12]1	▓		[13]2	[14]5	
8	▓	[15]1	1	0	[16]2			6	
▓	▓	8		0	[17]1	[18]3	[19]2	▓	
[20]4	[21]9	▓	[22]6	▓	[23]4		[24]6	4	▓
▓	9	[25]3	[26]5	[27]7	▓		[28]3		
[29]4	[30]0	▓	[31]4	[32]8	▓		[33]4	5	
[34]2	7	[35]9		8		[36]2	8	▓	

[1]4	[2]9	▓	[3]1	[4]8	▓	[5]6	[6]4	▓	[7]7
[8]2		▓	[9]2	1	▓	[10]3	5		2
▓	[11]5	4		[12]2	▓		[13]6		
[14]5	6	[15]2		[16]8	1		[17]3	[18]6	
0	▓	[19]2	4	▓		[20]3		4	
▓	[21]4	8		[22]1	[23]5	▓	[24]2	0	▓
[25]4	2	▓	[26]3		[27]6	[28]3	▓		[29]6
[30]8	▓	[31]1	6	▓		[32]2	[33]5		0
▓	[34]3	0	[35]2	[36]7		[37]6	[38]3	▓	
[39]4	[40]5		[41]0		[42]2	4		[43]5	4

[1]1	6	▓	[2]3	[3]5	▓	[4]2	4	▓	[5]1
2	▓	▓	[6]2	0	▓	8	▓	▓	4
▓	[7]2	7	▓		[8]1		[9]4	▓	
[10]3	0	▓	[11]1	▓	[12]2	0	▓	[13]2	[14]1
6	▓	[15]2	4	▓		[16]1			8
▓	[17]3	5	▓	[18]1	[19]4	▓	[20]5	4	
[21]1	6	▓	[22]3		0	▓		[23]2	
2	▓	[24]1	0	▓		[25]4	[26]5		7
▓	[27]1	4	▓	[28]3	[29]2		[30]4	[31]8	
[32]2	8	▓	[33]9		1			[34]8	

Maths

Co-ordinate Pictures

 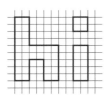 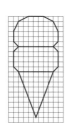   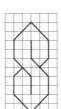 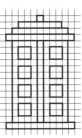

Prime Numbers

The grid with the prime numbers marked in colour can be found on Resource Sheet 2 on the CD-ROM. The children will be expected to find the following prime numbers according to their ability.

SEN

2, 3, 5, 7, 11, 13, 17, 19, 23, 29, 31, 37, 41, 43, 47

LA

53, 59, 61, 67, 71, 73, 79, 83, 89, 97

MA

101, 103, 107, 109, 113, 127, 131, 137, 139, 149

AA

151, 157, 163, 167, 173, 179, 181, 191, 193, 197, 199

Symbols Puzzles

Introduction: Figure 1

⚑	= 6
✉	= 8
◎	= 10
☺	= 5

Introduction: Figure 2

D	= 8
☒	= 4
✂	= 6
⌘	= 7

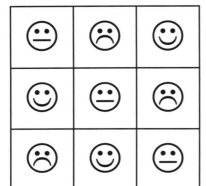

Maths

Symbols Puzzles (continued)

✉	=	8
⚑	=	6
◎	=	5
☺	=	4

$\boxtimes^2 - 1 = 80$, so $\boxtimes = 9$

$⚑ \times 5 + 3 = 43$, so $⚑ = 8$

$(◎ + 5) \times 2 = 24$, so $◎ = 7$

$(☺ \times 10) \div 2 = 30$, so $☺ = 6$

✉	✉	☺	✉	33
✉	☺	☺	⚑	29
☺	✉	✉	◎	31
⚑	☺	◎	◎	28
32	30	28	31	

Clock This!

1	1:28am
2	1:25pm
3	07:30
4	11pm
5	2:54am
6	21:25
7	4:20pm
8	00:00
9	20:15
10	5:26pm
11	00:45
12	18:30
13	15:29
14	7:50pm
15	13:15
16	7.00pm
17	15:10
18	22:25
19	16:05
20	Midnight
21	12:30
22	5:45am
23	8:20pm

1	17:45
2	6hrs 40mins
3	2hrs 5mins
4	11:25pm
5	16hrs 30mins
6	01:00
7	07:10
8	21:20
9	13:45
10	02:00
11	10:00
12	3hrs 20mins
13	07:35
14	20:55
15	05:50
16	7hrs 5mins
17	15:05
18	17:55
19	23hrs 40mins
20	23:20
21	10:00am (day before)
22	3hrs 20mins
23	19:30

	A	B
1	17:45	18:25
2	6hrs 40mins	2hrs 20mins
3	2hrs 5mins	13:40
4	11:25pm	06:30 & 23:25
5	16hrs 30mins	16:50
6	01:00	01:33
7	07:10	3hrs 55mins
8	21:20	01:25
9	13:45	13:20
10	02:00	06:40
11	10:00	04:00
12	3hrs 20mins	05:20
13	07:35	13:55
14	20:55	4hrs 5mins
15	05:50	18:50
16	7hrs 5mins	3hrs 35mins
17	15:05	13:05
18	17:55	GMT 1hr behind
19	23hrs 40mins	17:35 (next day)
20	23:20	18:20
21	10:00am (day before)	pm (14:30)
22	3hrs 20mins	02:50
23	19:30	9:30pm = 21:30

Literacy

Call My Bluff

agitate	a	stir up public interest, campaign
brier	a	a thorny bush
clamour	a	a loud, confused noise
cocotte	b	small fireproof dish for cooking and serving
confer	a	have a discussion
conspiracy	b	planning with others to do something illegal
cudgel	b	a short, thick stick used as a weapon
glutinous	c	glue-like or sticky
gore	a	to wound with a sharp object
hindquarters	c	an animal's hind legs and rear parts
hydrangea	a	a shrub with pink, blue or white flowers
hydrofoil	b	a boat designed to skim water
hypocrite	b	someone who goes against their word
lepidopterous	b	a type of butterfly or moth
lorgnette	b	a pair of spectacles held on a long handle
menagerie	a	a small zoo
monocle	a	a lens worn over one eye
orris	c	a violet-scented iris root used in perfumery
pict	a	a member of an ancient tribe of Scotland
poach	b	hunt animals illegally
poise	c	balance
receptacle	b	something for holding what is put into it
remnant	c	a small piece of something left over
remorse	c	deep regret for having done wrong
sonata	b	a piece of music for one or two instruments
syntax	c	the way words are arranged
transliterate	a	write a word in the letters of a different alphabet or language
trivial	b	not valuable
uranium	a	a heavy grey metal used as a source of nuclear energy
yield	c	an amount produced by something

Literacy

Perfect Punctuation

1. I have a little grey kitten called Smoky.
2. She is very mischievous and always getting into trouble.
3. One day I found Smoky stuck high up in a tree.
4. "Mum! Can you help me to get Smoky down?" I called.
5. "Oh dear!" exclaimed Mum. "How are we ever going to get her down?"
6. Just then, our window cleaner appeared.
7. "Can you help us to rescue our kitten?" pleaded Mum.
8. The window cleaner placed his huge ladder against the tree.
9. He carefully climbed up, grasped Smoky and carried her down to me.
10. As I cuddled her, she suddenly jumped out of my arms and back up the tree!

1. The door, which was ajar, slammed shut suddenly.
2. Bradley, who was the driver, stopped the car at the traffic lights, which were red.
3. "Eating five portions of fruit and vegetables," stated Mum, "is important to keep your body healthy."
4. "As soon as I get home," whinged Jay, "I'm getting out my Xbox."
5. In autumn, when the leaves fall off the trees, it is chilly and often windy.
6. The baby, who could not sleep, was crying throughout the night.
7. Craig and Gemma, who were brother and sister, fought like cat and dog.
8. The wind, which had begun to die down, suddenly blew up again, causing the leaves in the trees to tremble.

After break, the class sat on the carpet. Our teacher explained that we were going to have a discussion about what we did at the weekend.

"What did you do, Kiera?" she asked me.

"Well, I went to the park with my friends, Laura and Dean. We were going to play on the swings, but when we arrived Dean spotted a kitten struggling to climb down from a very high branch in a huge oak tree. It was mewing pitifully. 'Oh, listen to that poor little mite,' remarked Dean. 'Let's call the fire brigade to rescue it.' 'We don't need the fire brigade,' boasted Laura. 'I'm going to climb up and rescue it.' Laura began the long and difficult climb. She very nearly lost her footing several times. After a while, she finally reached the stranded kitten. She reached across to grasp it and the kitten immediately jumped to the ground and ran swiftly off. 'Guys!' wailed Laura, 'I'm stuck! I can't get down.' So we had to call the fire brigade after all!"

Simply Solar!

1. Such a high concentration of asteroids are found in that area.
2. Because it returns after periods of 75-76 years.
3. Pieces of rock and iron.
4. Between a few metres and 1000km.
5. Ice, dust and rock.
6. False. It is a star.
7. Because of the heat from the Sun.
8. Ice.
9. The coma.
10. A meteoroid that doesn't burn up completely
11. False. It is gas.
12. Kilometres.
13. It was named after Edmond Halley who, in 1705, predicted that Halley's comet would return in 1758, which it did – unfortunately, after he had died.
14. b) China
15. Small bits of material that fly through space.
16. Friction with the air.
17. 240BC.
18. They are so big and hit so fast and hard.
19. Iron.
20. 50 000 years ago.
21. c) billions
22. Meteors.
23. metre, meet, room, dome, dime, deem, trim, door, dire, mood, meted, meteor, doom, deem, tire, tired, rodeo, meter, mode, reed, deer, moor, ride, rode, reed, moored – and more!

Music

Vivaldi

Comparing Vivaldi's 'Four Seasons' Spring and Winter Concertos

	Spring	**Winter**
tempo	lively, fast, invigorating, exciting	calming, slow, gently washing over your ears, mellow, relaxing, sleepily
timbre	jolly, jerky, playful, cheeky, stirring, bracing	mellow, smooth
dynamics	gets louder, then quieter, then louder in each phrase	like speaking when your breath runs out at end of phrase/sentence
structure	beginning repeated, middle – end is beginning + new melodies ostinati of different melodies throughout	beginning and end repetition of melody and beat